Pushing the Boundaries In Christ

Living Supernaturally

Tony Myers

ISBN: 978-1-660774-62-3

Scripture quotations marked KJV are from the King James Version public domain

Scripture quotations marked TPT are from The Passion Translation®. Copyright © 2017, 2018 by Passion & Fire Ministries, Inc. Used by permission. All rights reserved. ThePassionTranslation.com

Scripture quotations marked NLT are taken from the *Holy Bible*, New Living Translation, copyright © 1996, 2004, 2015 by Tyndale House Foundation. Used by permission of Tyndale House Publishers, Inc., Carol Stream, Illinois 60188. All rights reserved

Quotations marked Jubilees are taken from the book of Jubilees public domain.

Quotations marked Enoch are taken from the book of Enoch public domain.

Quotations marked Jasher are taken from the book of Jasher public domain.

Dedication

This book is dedicated to my wife Debra Myers, without her faithful witness of Jesus Christ I may have never survived or become the believer in Christ that I am today.

This book is also dedicated to those who have gone on to their heavenly reward, before their time.

To my faithful readers that Holy Spirit will, as they read my books, give his revelation knowledge to them.

Table of Contents

Acknowledgements

Our Heavenly Father, Jesus Christ and the Holy Spirit are the reason for this book. Without whom there would be no reason for this book to be written. Nor would this author have attained the knowledge contained within these pages without them. Many thanks also go to those who took the time to read the book as the rough draft was being written. Tess Sainz, Chuck Barchuck, Peg Spicknall, and Shelley Smith. Thank you all for the encouragement.

Foreword

This special book you are holding in your hands or listening to is truly Supernatural. In fact, the author was healed of an incurable and terminal disease (that amazing story is in another book that I would highly recommend.) Getting back to this book, I propose that you devour it, savor it, but more than anything else plant these seeds contained herein into your heart, let them grow AND I guarantee you will see the Supernatural power of GOD (through Christ) work wonders and miracles in your life DAILY! People seek the supernatural – naturally… and as a seeker you will find this book to be a great source of wisdom and biblical proof that the Supernatural is for you… yes, right HERE and right NOW. I loved this book and wish I had access to it years ago! I believe you will feel the same way and there is no time like the present.

As a youngster growing up in the church, I never saw very many miracles, even though there was a list of people asking for prayer every week. The Minister would read the long list of requests to the congregation. We would then, as a group pray together, but I don't think many believed that it would actually work, and most were praying along simply to be kind. Just as you probably guessed, nothing happened. A miracle was almost non-existent, yet the Bible was full of supernatural miracles. We were all saved and going to heaven, but… simply believed that the supernatural happened in the Bible and Heaven only. Yes, certain ministers had special gifts, but these were far and few in between and this "supernatural stuff" was not for the common person.

As I got older and would pray, I wondered if GOD would perform miracles through me and any other common folks who were interested. True, I was not an elite minister but started thinking what did they have that I was missing? Also, what about scripture? What about the verses that say:

10 "I have come to give you everything in abundance more than you expect – life in its fullness until you overflow!" (John 10:10 The Passion)

6 "And because we are his children, God has sent the Spirit of his Son into our hearts, prompting us to call out, "Abba, Father." **7** Now you are no longer a slave but God's own child. And since you are his child, God has made you his heir. (Galatians 4:6-7, NLT)

As the truth of the matter started to sink in, I figured out that all I needed was to know the truth. That is what I was missing and the supernatural is for right here, right now and is RIGHT for ME. We are all heirs, which means we have access to everything now.

Once I learned some of these truths (they are all contained in this book and much, much more), some amazing miracles began to happen in my life. Here are just a few examples. Several years ago, I prayed for a relative, who was like a second mother to me. She was literally on her deathbed, dying of cancer. She was sent home to enjoy the last few days of her life. I knew that GOD could and would heal her and prayed with her for just that. Guess what? She was and is completely healed to this day and has been completely healthy for almost a decade. On another occasion, I met a stranger while getting my hair done at the salon. She was almost completely bent over, had tears in her eyes and was in excruciating pain. I inquired about her situation and she said she was scheduled for back surgery in a week. Without even thinking, I asked her if she wanted to be healed and we prayed together. Guess what? She was instantly healed (even I was surprised) and two weeks later she contacted my hairdresser again to make sure I knew that she did not need surgery any longer. WOW! All I did was ask GOD for help and command that her back be healed. It was a simple two sentence prayer. One time, when we first started our company, we were in need of a significant amount of cash quickly and my husband and I sat down and begin to pray. Within minutes FedEx was at the door delivering an overnight envelope containing a check for $250,000 from a client we had just started a relationship with. I thought WOW! That was a quick answer to prayer! When I called the client to tell her thank you, to my surprise she said I don't understand how you received a check from us. Number one, we never overnight payment and number two we only pay 30 days after completion. Now, I really started to pray and thought, "Will I have to send this check back?" Such little faith. She said, "Keep the check and I trust that you will do a good job. Again, I don't know how in the world you received our check but have a great day and you do not need to send it back." I've also had debt erased supernaturally, simply by hearing about GOD doing this for another and understanding that if he does this for anyone else, he will do it for you. Many of these truths I had to sleuth out on my own to see and understand that the supernatural is for all of GOD's children. The reason this book is so helpful is that it proves in a very detailed fashion that the supernatural is available to all every day of your life on earth. You will see that you can truly live in Heaven on Earth today!

Tony, thank you for being led to write this amazing and life-changing book and thank you for inviting me to celebrate it with you. You and your wife are such a blessing! Your other books on healing are life changing as well and I've sent them to so many friends to convey the Love of GOD and his desire to heal every person.

Shelley Smith. President & CEO

EPIC Worldwide LLC

PS - This book may be enjoyed even more with a hot cup of coffee or a latte.

Preface

The ultimate goal of every one of my books is for the reader to grow in reliance on Holy Spirit. It is for you, my friends, to be blessed, be healed and to be a blessing. We must grow until all of our brothers and sisters in Christ have reached the stature of Christ. This means that we walk as Jesus did, as a son of God. We have barely scratched the surface.

In my journey, the biggest hindrance I've seen in others is the lack of a renewed mind. Many people stay to the confined boundaries of this physical world not even considering there is so much more available to us in this lifetime. This leads to a lifetime of bad things happening to us and we develop a lifestyle of reacting to circumstances, the emergency response to those things.

We often develop a victim mindset living our lives, not as more than conquerors, but waiting for the next shoe to fall. Nearly every single person in the world has this mentality to some degree. We as humans become conformed to this world and a slave to physical circumstances. Which leads us to fighting health issue after health issue, financial restraints, and heartbreaking relationship failures. Abundant life doesn't even appear to be a blip on the radar. Yet, Jesus came so we could have life, and have it more abundantly.

In my first book on divine healing "Unlocking the Mystery of Divine Healing," I cover the foundation for divine healing. This book has opened many to the realization of how available Jesus and the Heavenly Father made healing. In "Divine Healing DIY," we get deeper into this subject.

Then came the mind-blowing book, "Knocking Food off its Pedestal." This book pushed people past their comfort zones and many people have been able to acknowledge their healing through these books. Thank you, Jesus! Yet, the one thing that I've continued to notice is that few are able to transition that into a more than a conqueror lifestyle through Jesus. This is where this book comes in.

You now know the fundamentals of healing, even if you are still struggling with symptoms. I confidently expect that if you are in this situation, then with this book you will be able to acknowledge your full healing and move way past that struggle into a supernatural lifestyle.

Most people start off their Journey with Christ through religion which constricts, strangles, and manipulates. The supernatural isn't even on the radar with religion. Then at some point they realize walking in Christ isn't about religious traditions and how they've been misled and filled with a bunch of wrong teachings. They find healing and what a real relationship is with The Father and Jesus.

Most people start seeing miracles to some degree either in themselves or in others. Yet, their way of thinking stays conformed to the physical boundaries of this physical world. It is time to totally renew our thinking to what we are In Christ and to bust through the physical barriers of this world and truly start living in the supernatural.

In God's Kingdom, we are now sons and daughters of the One True Living God. We need to start thinking in our daily lives, not as mere mortals who are under physical limitations, but as sons and daughters who have no natural boundaries.

It still amazes me that many of my friends and those in the body of Christ who have seen the wonderful fruits of the Holy Spirit are still bound by the physical limitations of this world. I'm talking about people who, like me, have seen the dead raised, legs grow out, spinal cord injuries healed, and many other amazing things.

Yet, they are still held bondage by food, physical injuries, allergies, etc.

It is time to push the boundaries and to, quite frankly, get over it. It is time to become more reliant on the Holy Spirit and less reliant on the physical nature of physical things. We as sons of God are meant to interact with the physical world not to be constrained by the physical world and its limitations. That's what this book is about.

Ok, this is where my disclaimer comes in… not the normal disclaimer: I am not talking about submerging yourself into the "spiritual world" of seeing angels, talking to angels, relying on angels to do the supernatural things. Angels are real, but that kind of thing isn't what this book is about.

Too many people go from religion into peering into the spiritual world and becoming infatuated with angels and demons. Many times, when I say the word supernatural, people think I'm referring to angels and demons. I'm not. This book isn't about communicating with angels, rather what we ourselves are capable of with reliance on Holy Spirit who is in us, not reliance on angels.

I am not discounting angels, or that there is some interaction with them in our kingdom lifestyle. However, I find those who give the most wonderful accounts of experiences with angels are just as sickly and oppressed as those who don't.

The key to pushing the physical boundaries doesn't rely on or require interaction with the unseen world of angels. In fact, those who constantly talk about angels have lives that are often more reliant upon the constrictive nature of the physical world than those who don't. Renewing our minds to the fullness of Christ has nothing to do with angelic beings. Let them do as Our Lord Jesus Christ has commanded them to do, but let's leave well enough alone.

It should be noted that throughout this book there is content taken from three ancient texts that are mentioned in scriptures as authoritative. These are the books of Enoch, Jasher, and Jubilees. The author considers them to be legitimate historical books that fill in a lot of information not found elsewhere.

One last point to make and it's about my third favorite subject: Yes, coffee! I've been criticized about how I mention coffee all the time, in my books. Well if that seems cheesy or disconcerting to you, I do apologize. Get over it! That's just me and how I write. If you write a book, you're allowed to include your interests. So, I'll include mine. Speaking of which, my cup is empty. Time to fill'er up as we get ready to dive into the first chapter

1. Defining the Mind of Adam

"Please God heal me this one time and I'll scream it from the mountain tops and serve you forever." "God, I beg you this one time. Send me a financial miracle." "God, if you get me out of this problem, I'll never miss church again." That is how so many people experience God. When things look bad, we cry out and beg and plead for a miracle that never seems to come.

Or, we get that once in a lifetime experience and keep it to ourselves. Some may share it with just a few friends. Eventually, we pretty much forget about it.

There's a third group with increasing numbers, those who see many miracles in others yet can't quite seem to have that one for themselves. The last group of people are those who are seeing miracles for themselves and others and walking in a pretty solid arena of divine health and abundance. They're a rare group of people. But even in this group, our numbers are increasing. Only a small number of people walk fully in divine healing for themselves and others.

It doesn't matter which group you're in. We all need to push the boundaries to reach the next level of where the human race should be In Christ. The next level is the body of Christ as a whole, reaching a whole new level of "not conforming to this world" in every area of life. This means that the nation of Christ is finally viewed as a peculiar people whom everyone wants to be a part of. They are healthier, happier, and more loving than any other type of people.

We aren't there yet. The reason why is because we are still living and thinking by the boundaries set at the garden, by God to Adam. We are still thinking like mere mortals here on earth just to toil all our lives till we die and get to heaven. We haven't come to the true revelation of what and who we are In Christ. We may confess to be In Christ, but we're living our lives in Adam.

Before defining what is meant by being and thinking like Adam, let's address a group of people that will argue with me and say, "Tony I'm a seer. I see into the spiritual world. I see angels all around me. I know who I am in Christ." "Tony, I've seen many miracles. I prophesy. I know who I am In Christ." "I get slain in the spirit every Sunday. I walk around feeling the presence of God all around me." "I see and talk to angels. I've visited heaven a number of times. Jesus and I talk every day." "I've had gold dust appear on my hands. Jewels have just appeared out of nowhere. I live ""in the spirit'."

The intention is not to make fun of those things. But then the question has to be asked, "How is your life in this world?" If you're walking in divine health, and your relationships are wonderful, and all your needs are met, then why did you even buy this book?

Maybe you are still searching for something. The truth is this: We may be experiencing these things, but have we truly renewed our minds to the Truth we have In Christ?

If you are still struggling with medical issues, then you may have renewed your mind to "the spirit world," but are still bound to physical limitations. Then, is your mind truly renewed? There are a huge number of people who operate in the "spiritual gifts." Yet, their minds and actions are still carnal. By carnal it is meant controlled by our physical senses. For the record, I'm right there with everyone else, still renewing my mind. Let's now define what is meant by the phrase "Mind of Adam" or being "In Adam."

> **15** And I will cause hostility between you and the woman, and between your offspring and her offspring. He will strike your head, and you will strike his heel." **16** Then he said to the woman, "I will sharpen the pain of your pregnancy, and in pain you will give birth. And you will desire to control your husband, but he will rule over you."**17** And to the man he said, "Since you listened to your wife and ate from the tree whose fruit, I commanded you not to eat, the ground is cursed because of you. All your life you will struggle to scratch a living from it. **18** It will grow thorns and thistles for you, though you will eat of its grains. **19** By the sweat of your brow will you have food to eat until you return to the ground from which you were made. For you were made from dust, and to dust you will return." (Genesis 3:15-19, NLT)

This is where man became a physical being or where the physical nature of man was born. "The human condition" came upon mankind, and death came into this world. This is where the physical boundaries and physical laws were put into place. Time became a measured number. Mankind became a slave to seconds, minutes, hours, days, weeks, months and years. Space became measured by gravity for every step people took the law of gravity put up resistance limiting how far a person could travel. Mankind was then subject to injury, disease, the elements of weather, and then death. Adam and Eve went from spiritual beings who lived in a physical body without any limitations, to becoming mere mortals subject to the physical laws of a natural Earth. Think of it this way, Adam and Eve had "glorified bodies," they lived from their spirit and simply used their physical bodies to interact with the world. Then, with the fruit they became spirits trapped in a physical body that was subjected to the physical nature of things. It is often taught that man's spirit died. I do not see scriptural evidence of this. Rather mankind's spirit became dulled. We lost our identity of being born of God's image.

With being under the physical nature of things, Adam and Eve had to learn how to exist in the natural world which meant solving physical problems with a physical solution. To cover themselves, they had to use a fig leaf. Then, God showed them how to make clothes from animal skins. Now, let's take a look at some traits of the mind of Adam:

1. Assumes the worst.
2. Fears being hurt (emotional or physical) or dying.
3. Self-preservation/selfish.
4. Looks to solve a problem with a physical solution.
5. Never considers a supernatural solution.
6. Forgets past experiences where there is a supernatural solution.

The mind of Adam is sensitive to negative circumstances and expects the worst. The most apparent example of this is Abraham when he tells Pharaoh that Sarah is his sister:

> "Whatever possessed you to do such a thing?" Abraham replied, "I thought, 'This is a godless place. They will want my wife and will kill me to get her." (Genesis 20:10-11, NLT)

Abraham is in fear of his life without cause. His first thought goes to being killed, not even considering Sarah's well-being. Let's remember this: The Old Testament happens before Christ! It is all happening during the time that all of mankind is born into the sin of Adam, prior to the day of Pentecost. With this in mind, there are many examples of this in the Old Testament scriptures.

In this example with Abraham, he exhibits all of the five traits of the mind of Adam. He assumes the worst. He thinks out the physical solution even before there is a need, which means he is in fear, and never even considers trusting God for a solution. He also fails to consider past events in which God had intervened. The thought of trusting God for his safety never even enters into his thoughts. In fact, after this situation he makes the same mistake again even though God had intervened. This is passed down to his son Isaac as he makes the same errors his father made.

All throughout the Old Testament scriptures, this pattern repeats itself continuously. Esau, a hunter, comes back from a hunting trip. Evidently, it's an unsuccessful one. He is starving to death and gives up his birthright for a meal. On the surface level, who wouldn't have done the same thing?

Jacob withholds food from his starving brother to receive a physical solution, and it seems that Esau, in order to live, takes an appropriate action. While reading this story in scriptures, I'm always thinking, "God, get Jacob! He's so wicked!" Yet, the story always ends up the same. God siding with Jacob.

> **29** One day when Jacob was cooking some stew, Esau arrived home from the wilderness exhausted and hungry. **30** Esau said to Jacob, "I'm starved! Give me some of that red stew!" (This is how Esau got his other name, Edom, which means "red.") **31** "All right," Jacob replied, "but trade me your rights as the firstborn son." **32** "Look, I'm dying of starvation!" said Esau. "What good is my birthright to me now?" **33** But Jacob said, "First you must swear that your birthright is mine." So, Esau swore an oath, thereby selling all his rights as the firstborn to his brother, Jacob. **34** Then Jacob gave Esau some bread and lentil stew. Esau ate the meal, then got up and left. He showed contempt for his rights as the firstborn. (Genesis 25:29-34, NLT)

> **13** In the words of the Scriptures, "I loved Jacob, but I rejected Esau." (Romans 9:13, NLT)

Esau feared dying, looked to resolve the problem on his own, never considered a supernatural solution, and did not use any past experiences he had with God. We do know from scripture that God had chosen Jacob, but my points are still valid. These and the many other examples show us the condition of the human race when we were in Adam.

We've looked at Abraham, the father of our faith, whose lineage brought us our Savior, Jesus Christ. Let's look at other great chosen men of God.

Elijah was no doubt one of the greatest prophets of God with many supernatural experiences. Even with all his experiences with God, he reacted many times with the mind of Adam. For example, he fled from Jezebel out of fear, and never even thought of supernatural intervention in that instance.

Another prime example of the mind of Adam is the children of Israel in the desert. They were all involved in miracle after miracle, their clothes and shoes did not wear out, and there were no feeble among them. They had seen the parting of the Red Sea, walked on solid land where there had been nothing but water, and witnessed all of Egypt's soldiers destroyed. Yet, still they constantly grumbled and complained even accusing God of leading them into the desert to let them die of hunger and thirst.

God then sent them manna and quail. Even while receiving this food, they once again complained of dying from thirst. This is an entire nation made up of over a million people who constantly overlooked God as a supernatural provider while in the middle of experiencing supernatural provision. There were only two that we know of that never complained Aaron and Moses.

Every single person on this earth can relate to the mind of Adam. None of this comes as a shock to anyone. This chapter isn't a life changing revelation of itself. The reason why we all have this same experience is because we relate easier to the mind of Adam. We're still stuck with the mindset that we are, after all, only human. So, we go from struggle to struggle, we face difficult circumstance after difficult circumstance and get beat down because we think that we are still under the restrictions and boundaries that were spelled out after Adam took the fruit of the tree of knowledge.

Let's take note of a few things here. All of the examples above are of those who were still under the first Adam. Even though they were still under the first Adam's sentence, they still experienced the supernatural including miracles. This was long before Jesus came.

Spiritual things did not just leave the world completely when Adam was thrown out of the garden. We compartmentalize the spiritual world and think that it is separate from the physical world. This is a huge error on our part. That error is also why the supernatural seems to be hit and miss or a once in a lifetime experience.

The physical world is not separate from the spiritual world, rather the very fabric of which the physical world is made is from the spiritual world. It is not possible to separate the physical world from the spiritual because the physical nature of things then dissolves into nothing. The physical world does not exist without the spiritual world. Therefore, the supernatural is always an option.

> **1** Faith shows the reality of what we hope for; it is the evidence of things we cannot see. **2** Through their faith, the people in days of old earned a good reputation. **3** By faith we understand that the entire universe was formed at God's command, that what we now see did not come from anything that can be seen. (Hebrews 11:1-3, NLT)

> **17** He existed before anything else, and he holds all creation together. (Colossians 1:17, NLT)

Therefore, to think that there is a separation between the physical and spiritual is a wrong belief. The only separation is that one is seen, and one is unseen. It is the unseen that binds the physical world together. I know that messes with a lot of people's theology, which is always a great thing since it was Christ who gave us the example of pushing wrong theological boundaries.

Let's look at the disciples before the cross while Jesus was with them in a physical body. They were still in the first Adam at that point but were surrounded daily and hourly by His miracles and they, themselves, were performing miracles. Yet, they had amnesia when it came to the miraculous.

They saw Jesus turn water into wine. Yet, when it came to feeding the crowds of thousands, it didn't occur to them that Jesus could multiply food. At that moment, the supernatural wasn't even a blip on their radar. Then, came the food miracle with food to spare.

Next, their boat is caught up in a storm. Jesus has to run and calm the storm because they were losing their minds thinking they were gonna die! He then points out that their hearts were hardened because they hadn't even entertained the thought that the storm could be calmed. After they went through that, there was another storm, and once again they were terrified for their lives. Do you see how forgetful the mindset of Adam is?

Just as the nation of Israel during the Exodus lived in the miraculous, the disciples did too, and guess what? They meet all the criteria for the mind of Adam.

The Adam minded person knows only the physical realities of things. He is controlled by his environment and is under the restrictions of the physical world. He knows and lives by what his physical senses and experiences have shown him. There are different levels of the Adam nature, yet there is a victim mentality to it. The Adam mind thinks we are at the mercy of the realities of the physical world and forgets that we were created in God's image. In other words, just as Adam and Eve lost sight of the fact that God made them perfect, the mind of Adam has an identity crisis as well. The mind of Adam rationalizes supernatural experiences as well just chalking them up to coincidence or minimizes them to something insignificant.

Worksheet: Chapter 1

1. What are the six traits of the mind of Adam?

2. Think about the day you've experienced today. Which traits did you portray today?

3. I contend that the supernatural is experienced every day. We just fail to recognize it. Name one instance of the supernatural that occurred in your life today.

4. Search scripture out for yourself: I make the statement that man's spirit did not die after the fall. Can you prove that I'm wrong? If so, list at least two scriptures supporting your opinion.

5. Name one incident of a great man of God, succumbing to the mind of Adam.

____
____
____
____

6. In your own words, what can you use as a red flag to be able to recognize when you're operating in Adam's Nature?

____
____
____
____

NOTES:

____
____
____
____

2. Physical Authority

We need to establish the types of authority and powers that exist since there is much confusion over this. There is spiritual authority and there is physical authority. Let's discuss physical authority first.

> **26** Then God said, "Let us make human beings in our image, to be like us. They will reign over the fish in the sea, the birds in the sky, the livestock, all the wild animals on the earth, and the small animals that scurry along the ground." **27** So God created human beings in his own image. In the image of God he created them; male and female he created them. **28** Then God blessed them and said, "Be fruitful and multiply. Fill the earth and govern it. Reign over the fish in the sea, the birds in the sky, and all the animals that scurry along the ground." (Genesis 1:26-28, NLT)

> **16** The heavens belong to the Lord, but he has given the earth to all humanity. (Psalm 115:16, NLT)

This, for some reason, is the hardest concept for us to grasp. God in his great wisdom was actually protecting mankind, by giving us authority over the Earth. Human authority was never transferred to an angelic power.

It is often taught that through the fall, man gave his authority over to the devil, Satan, or Lucifer. This is not the case. It is also taught that the devil has abilities on the Earth. That by eating the fruit, Adam's authority was transferred to the devil. Therefore, demons now have the "spiritual authority" to affect mankind. Because of this, we are taught that witchcraft uses spiritual/demonic authority to afflict people. This isn't true at all. Witchcraft is a use or misuse of man's physical authority, to which we give the credit to demons, the devil, or other spiritual entities we believe exist. The explanation for that will be revealed over the next few chapters.

There is a purpose for this chapter. The Father wants believers to walk in power. Believers fear the supernatural. Those with hardened hearts don't. Throughout all of history there is a double side to everything. Hence the tree of knowledge of good and evil. Any object or action on the face of the earth can either be viewed as good or evil or both, this depends solely on the person and their perspective on the object or action. This often leads Believers of Christ to inaction, doubt, or full-blown fear of the supernatural. Often, religion and its leaders paint a fearful picture of the supernatural to keep those below them in obedience.

Did you realize that anything repeated enough eventually becomes a mainstream belief, even when it has no factual basis? A good example of this is coffee. People have been told all their lives that coffee dehydrates. As a result, you have to drink extra water when you drink coffee. A large majority of people believe that. In fact, I submit the only ones that don't believe that are the ones that experience the truth for themselves. I have drunk coffee all my life and, despite well-meaning people warning me to drink water, I haven't. When I prove the truth by showing how elastic my skin is, they rationalize this away, simply dismissing it and going along with their life still believing the lie. With that being the case, in order for you to believe the truth, an airtight case has to be built, one that leaves no wiggle room for you to rationalize the truth away.

The statement in chapter one that the spiritual things cannot be separated from the physical things is true. That being the case, man's physical authority is spiritual, but it can only be accessed by flesh and blood. It takes a physical person for something to happen on this Earth. Even God obeys this. He is the one who established the physical law. Which is one reason why Jesus had to come as a man.

From the beginning of scriptures to the end when we're talking about supernatural experiences, what is the one common denominator? That is correct! Flesh and blood are involved in each. A physical being was involved in Moses parting the Red Sea, for example. Let's take a close look at that.

> **13** But Moses told the people, "Don't be afraid. Just stand still and watch the Lord rescue you today. The Egyptians you see today will never be seen again. **14** The Lord himself will fight for you. Just stay calm." (Exodus 14:13-14, NLT)

Moses is telling the people to just stand still and wait for God to fight for them. But he did not fully understand the physical authority that God had given man. God proceeds to rebuke Moses and then spells out for him what to do.

> **15** Then the Lord said to Moses, "Why are you crying out to me? Tell the people to get moving! **16** Pick up your staff and

> raise your hand over the sea. Divide the water so the Israelites can walk through the middle of the sea on dry ground. (Exodus 14:15-16, NLT)

Don't dismiss this. You will find that often, God has to show us the authority that we are given on this Earth Himself. Does this scenario sound familiar? It should.

With the disciples, a similar scenario is played out. Jesus is sleeping and a storm rises up. The disciples are in fear of their lives. They wake up Jesus and he rebukes them as well.

> **23** Then Jesus got into the boat and started across the lake with his disciples. **24** Suddenly, a fierce storm struck the lake, with waves breaking into the boat. But Jesus was sleeping. **25** The disciples went and woke him up, shouting, "Lord, save us! We're going to drown!"**26** Jesus responded, "Why are you afraid? You have so little faith!" Then he got up and rebuked the wind and waves, and suddenly there was a great calm. (Matthew 8:23-26, NLT)

Why did Jesus rebuke them? It was because He expected them to calm the storm. In every single case where there is a supernatural occurrence, a person has to take an action. Even in the case when God was appointing Moses to go back to Egypt and get the Israelites free from the abuse of the Egyptians, it started with God instructing Moses to throw his staff on the ground. Only after he acted did it turn into a snake. Moses had to grab the tail of the snake for it to turn back into a staff. Later, God instructed Moses to put his hand into his cloak and his skin turned white. (Exodus 4:1-9) All throughout scriptures this is done. This is all done with man's physical authority over the Earth.

Look at the plagues of Egypt. In each case, God told Moses what to say. Moses had to speak it out. Even when it came to weather such as the hail, God told Moses to perform an action so that hail would fall from the sky (Exodus 9:22). We have an abundance of occasions of God telling a specific person to say and/or do specific things. Such as with Moses and the plagues of Egypt, we have the time in the desert where the children of Israel's clothes and shoes did not wear out, the manna from heaven, and the quail coming in the midst of the camp. Moses spoke in the physical, then the supernatural happened. In fact, I could recite all the miracles in scriptures, and you will find one commonality in every single case: a person had to perform an action or speak it out.

We really have no true realization of the physical authority that God gave to man. Even when it came to Jesus being born, God had the prophets speak everything out about His life. There is a two-fold reason for this: 1) So that all of mankind would know that Jesus is our King and Messiah, and 2) Because Jesus had to be spoken into existence.

The reason that Jesus had to be spoken into existence is because the children of Israel requested one person to represent them. They had the opportunity at Mount Sinai to be under the Covenant of Grace but refused. They didn't want to hear from God Himself and be solely under His rule. So, the Creator of the Universe who made all things including humankind, whom He created in his image, made one very special person so that His Will would be fulfilled.

> **15** Moses continued, "The Lord your God will raise up for you a prophet like me from among your fellow Israelites. You must listen to him. **16** For this is what you yourselves requested of the Lord your God when you were assembled at Mount Sinai. You said, 'Don't let us hear the voice of the Lord our God anymore or see this blazing fire, for we will die.' (Deuteronomy 18:15-16, NLT)

That is when God raised up prophets to speak prophesies of Jesus. Therefore, in every book of the Old Testament, Jesus is spoken about and into existence.

There could be no mistaking who Jesus was when the time for fulfillment had come. This is why Jesus had to be the Son of God and the Son of Man, so that everything would become as God had willed it.

Jesus had to be able to speak God's Word perfectly and have human physical and spiritual authority. Jesus was the only one to perfectly hear from God. When it comes to the supernatural, most people think that God just sovereignly decides to act, and that unless a voice comes down from heaven and tells you something directly, then it is wrong to expect it or, horror of all horrors, it is so wrong to command something to happen. That isn't the case. Here is an example:

> **12** On the day the Lord gave the Israelites victory over the Amorites, Joshua prayed to the Lord in front of all the people of Israel. He said, "Let the sun stand still over Gibeon, and the moon over the valley of Aijalon." **13** So the sun stood still and the moon stayed in place until the nation of Israel had defeated its enemies. Is this event not recorded in The Book of **Jashar**? The sun stayed in the middle of the sky, and it did not set as on a normal day. (Joshua 10:12-13, NLT)

Pay attention here and notice a couple of things. The text says Joshua prayed to the Lord in front of all the people. He didn't "pray" the way you think. He commanded the sun to stand still. Did he ask God for permission first? Where did God tell him to say this? The modern-day preacher would go up to Joshua and say, "Who are you to command that? Such blasphemy!" The board of elders would call an emergency meeting and reprimand Joshua.

Let's also look at the statement, "is this not recorded in the book of Jasher." The book of Jasher is mentioned, yet it is not in the modern-day Bible. In fact, it is mentioned as an authoritative book. Because of this, that book and two others also mentioned and quoted in scriptures are referenced to in this book. Those other two are the book of Enoch and Jubilees. Both are mentioned and quoted from in scriptures and they've got a lot to say about the supernatural.

The book of Jasher really shows how normal the supernatural lifestyle should be. The Heavenly Father loves us. Therefore, the supernatural power of our physical authority exists in our reality. The book of Jasher ties in much of the missing pieces that aren't in scriptures. This is my paraphrase of Jacob and his son Joseph from that book: When the sons of Jacob went home and told Jacob that his son was ripped apart by a wild beast. Jacob sent his sons back out to find the beast that had killed Joseph, supposedly. The brothers came upon a wolf and brought the wolf to Jacob. Holding the wolf in his hands Jacob asked why the beast had ripped him apart. The wolf answered Jacob!

> **44** "As God liveth who created us in the Earth, and as thy soul liveth, my lord, I did not see thy son, neither did I tear him to pieces, but from a distant land I also came to seek my son who went from me this day, and I know not whether he be living or dead." (Jasher, 43:44)

This wolf literally talked to Jacob after he had spoken out loud to the wolf! Yes, Jacob was amazed that the wolf responded. That is because man has never realized the amount of authority provided for them, especially those who have boundaries and wish to have morals. Those who are hard hearted don't have that dilemma. Why do you think that the Father hates those who are puffed up by their own pride and haughtiness? It is that they have no humility and use their authority to hurt, kill, and steal from others. They have no moral values to contain them. Let's look at Moses' life who from day one experienced miracle after miracle, many more than most are aware of.

At the age of three Moses was sitting on the lap of the Pharaoh's daughter during a banquet and reached over and grabbed the crown off the king's head and placed it on his own head. The king consulted Balaam in which he suggested to put a black onyx stone and a piece of coal burning in front of Moses. If the child grabbed the onyx stone, then he had performed that action out of wisdom and should be put to death. If he grabbed the piece of coal, then it was without wisdom and he should then live. Moses went to reach for the onyx stone, but an angel of the Lord intervened and placed Moses' hand on the coal and then put the coal to the child's lips in which his tongue was burnt off, from that time forward Moses was of heavy speech and stammered (Jasher 70, Paraphrased). If you ever wondered why Moses stammered, now you know.

There is much more. Another unknown detail is that after Moses fled Egypt, he went to the land of Cush and reigned for forty years as king (Jasher, Chapter 70, Paraphrased).

My whole point in showing these things is to point out how natural the supernatural should be. One could argue that this was Moses, who was handpicked and chosen by God, specifically. Yet, the sons of Jacob who sold Joseph into slavery were no strangers to the miraculous. Two of them, Simeon and Levi, leveled whole cities. They went to war against a city that had defiled their sister Dinah, totally destroying it between the two of them. The sons of Jacob destroyed over ten cities without an army. One thing to realize is the sons of Jacob were actually quite deceitful and by no means innocent themselves. But every time they requested of the Lord; their request was granted them based solely on who their father was. In fact, Jacob rebuked them for stirring up trouble. Yet, every time they faced a battle, they won and spread fear throughout the land of Caanan. What follows is an excerpt from the book of Jasher:

> **3** Are you silly this day or is there no understanding in you, that you will fight with the Hebrews, and why will you take a delight in your own destruction this day? **4** Behold two of them came to the city of Shechem without fear or terror, and they killed all the inhabitants of the city, that no man stood up against, and how will you be able to fight with them all? **5** Surely you know that their God is exceedingly fond of them, and has done mighty things for them, such as have not been done from days of old, and amongst all the gods of nations, there is none can do like unto his mighty deeds. (Jasher 35:3-5)

These are the wise men of the city reminding the citizens that it was foolish to stand up to them. The sons of Jacob had God on their side. This is how confident we should be in our Father in all situations:

> **6** Surely he delivered their father Abraham, the Hebrew, from the hand of Nimrod, and from the hand of all his people who had many times sought to slay him. **7** He delivered him also from the fire in which king Nimrod had cast him, and his God delivered him from it. **8** And who else can do the like? Surely it was Abraham who slew the five kings of Elam, when they had touched his brother's son who in those days dwelt in Sodom. (Jasher 35:6-8)

We as believers share in this legacy, and even a greater legacy. Yet, the counselors were not done in recounting how great the God of Abraham is.

> **9** And took his servant that was faithful in his house and a few of his men, and pursued the kings of Elam in one night

> and killed them, and restored to his brother's son all his property which they had taken from him. **10** And surely you know the God of these Hebrews is much delighted with them, and they are also delighted with him, for they know that he delivered them from all their enemies. (Jasher 35:9-10)

All of these deeds were so well known that even people that hadn't had direct contact with them knew how the faithful the God of Abraham is to those who love him.

> **11** And behold through his love toward his God, Abraham took his only and precious son and intended to bring him up as a burnt offering to his God, and had it not been for God who prevented him from doing this, he would then have done it through his love to his God. **12** And God saw all his works, and swore unto him, and promised him that he would deliver his sons and all seed from every trouble that would befall them, because he had done this thing, and through his love to his God stiffled his compassion for his child. **13** And have you not heard what their God did to Pharaoh king of Egypt, and Abimelech king of Gerar, through taking Abraham's wife, who said of her. She is my sister, lest they might slay him on account of her, and think of taking her for a wife? And God did unto them and their people all that you heard of. (Jasher 35:11-13)

In the following verses the counselors are telling them of what they knew firsthand how Abraham's brother Esau couldn't even withstand the sons of Jacob, because God was with them.

> **14** And behold, we ourselves saw with our eyes that Esau, the brother of Jacob, came to him with four hundred men, with the intention of slaying him, for he called to that he had taken away from him his father's blessing. **15** And he went

> to him when he came from Syria, to smite the mother with the children, and who delivered him from his hands but his God in whom he trusted? He delivered him from the hand hand of his brother and also from the hands of his and surely he again will protect them. **16** Who does not know that it was their God who inspired them with strength to do to the town of Shechem the evil which you heard of? **17** Could it then be with their own strength that two men could destroy such a large city as Shechem had it not been for their God in whom they trusted? He said and did unto them all this to slay the inhabitants of the city in their city. **18** And can you then prevail over them who have come forth together from your city to fight with the whole of them, even if a thousand times as many more should come to your assistance? **19** Surely you know and understand that you do not come to fight with them, but you come to war with their God who made choice of them, and you have therefore all come this day to be destroyed." (Jasher 35:14-19)

That is what the Ammorite counselors had to say, this was long before all the wonders done in Egypt with Moses. Long before the feats of Joshua, King David and all the like. Long before Jesus. This is our inheritance today as well In Christ we are the seed of Abraham, therefore heirs of the promise. Think about this and ponder on it. Our deeds as Christians should be known far and wide, in a peaceful loving context. Yet, no one is impressed when we say we are Christians.

> **29** And now that you belong to Christ, you are the true children of Abraham. You are his heirs, and God's promise to Abraham belongs to you. (Galatians 3:29, NLT)

This being the case we should be more accepting of a supernatural lifestyle and expecting miracles every day. We should then have the mindset of God was there for them so He's here for me. If the sons of Jacob who had their own brother sold into slavery, could experience miracles on a daily basis then we who are In Christ should have the mindset to experience even greater. Not to mention that often quoted, little believed scripture "greater things than these shall you do," which was from Jesus himself.

Worksheet: Chapter 2

1. Who was given authority on Earth?

___

2. In the Old Testament, how many times did a biblical figure act on his/her own without God telling them to command it and it happened? (This is to get you to study this out for yourself)

___

3. Why does God hate prideful people?

___

4. What is our lineage as believers in Christ?

___

5. Is it safe to assume, there were more miracles in the Old Testament than are recorded in our bibles? Why? (Trick question)

___

6. What is the definition of physical authority? Who can operate in physical authority?

7. Describe your favorite supernatural experience that you've had personally.

NOTES:

3. The Use of Physical Authority

All authority is spiritual in nature because it was given by God the creator of the universe who is a spirit. The spiritual things cannot be separated from the physical things or the physical things no longer exist. We're calling it physical authority only because it takes flesh and blood for things to happen on this Earth. God in His infinite wisdom made it this way. Because of this, the supernatural evil things that happen are not from the power of demons, rather from the physical authority of a person. For something to happen supernaturally it doesn't have to be authorized by God and demons don't have the authority or power to cause evil to happen. They never had that kind of authority on Earth.

Oh, I saw that look that you just gave me, but it's the truth. In this chapter, that's what we're going to explore. First, I'm going to show you that not everything that we think is done with God's approval is done with his approval at all. Rather, it is a person stepping out in his own will and using physical authority. Then, we're going to discuss how wicked things exist through physical authority, not angelic or demonic authority.

But first, for those of you that don't know, I love my coffee. We're going to take a moment and enjoy a caramel latte'. I know that just knocked some of you for a loop as I've always been a pure black coffee drinker. I was given an espresso machine, so I started exploring the world of the latte'. One time a day, a latte' is made and I've grown to enjoy it! This from the person that used to say that cream, sugar, and other additives are the abomination that causes desolation. Keep this on the hush and hush because if Diana finds out, I'll never hear the end of it. So, shush and don't tell no one!

Elijah the prophet of God performed many miracles. His supernatural lifestyle is one of historic value. Yet, as great as he was, there were still errors that he made. We think that every miracle he performed was approved by God and that isn't true. There's that look again. Wait till we get to Moses!

Let's talk about one specific event in Elijah's life. Here's when he called fire down from heaven on the two groups of soldiers sent by the king to escort him to the palace:

> **8** "Elijah from Tishbe!" the king exclaimed. **9** Then he sent an army captain with fifty soldiers to arrest him. They found him sitting on top of a hill. The captain said to him, "Man of God, the king has commanded you to come down with us." **10** But Elijah replied to the captain, "If I am a man of God, let fire come down from heaven and destroy you and your fifty men!" Then fire fell from heaven and killed them all. **11** So the king sent another captain with fifty men. The captain said to him, "Man of God, the king demands that you come down at once." **12** Elijah replied, "If I am a man of God, let

> fire come down from heaven and destroy you and your fifty men!" And again the fire of God fell from heaven and killed them all. (2 Kings 1:8-12, NLT)

Just because someone makes the statement of being a man of God, doesn't mean He endorses every action that the man of God makes. God didn't endorse Elijah's action to want to give up and die when Jezebel threatened him. Nor did He endorse Elijah hiding out in the caves in fear of his life. Fear is one indicator of whether it is of God or not.

In this instance of Elijah calling down fire from heaven, he was in fear for his life and thus was acting out of fear, not out of obedience to God. In this act, it took an angel to halt Elijah before he destroyed the third group of soldiers sent to get him.

> **13** Once more the king sent a third captain with fifty men. But this time the captain went up the hill and fell to his knees before Elijah. He pleaded with him, "O man of God, please spare my life and the lives of these, your fifty servants. **14** See how the fire from heaven came down and destroyed the first two groups. But now please spare my life!" **15** Then the angel of the Lord said to Elijah, "Go down with him, and don't be afraid of him." So, Elijah got up and went with him to the king. (2 Kings 1:13-15, NLT)

You see how the angel stated not to be afraid of him? Elijah was in fear, and the angel was sent to stop him from acting again. Many people will state that because the captain pleaded for mercy, that was the reason the angel came. But I beg to differ. Jesus' own words show us the truth about this. When the Samaritans were roughing up Jesus and the disciples, they wanted to do the same thing Elijah had done, call fire down from heaven. Jesus stopped them and stated you know not what spirit you are operating from. That spirit was fear, same as Elijah.

> **51** And it came to pass, when the time was come that he should be received up, he stedfastly set his face to go to Jerusalem, **52** and sent messengers before his face: and they went, and entered into a village of the Samaritans, to make ready for him. **53** And they did not receive him, because his face was as though he would go to Jerusalem. **54** And when his disciples James and John saw this, they said, Lord, wilt thou that we command fire to come down from heaven, and consume them, even as Elias did? **55** But he turned, and rebuked them, and said, Ye know not what manner of spirit ye are of. (Luke 9:51-55, KJV)

When we're talking about "they would not receive them," we aren't talking about a polite please leave our city. They were pushing, shoving, and getting physical with them which is why it is stated that James and John saw the violence. Essentially, it is the same event with Jesus showing the correct response. This is the very same Jesus who stated, "If you've seen me, you've seen the Father."

Then, we have Moses who acted outside of God's command to speak to the rock. Water still gushed forth, in spite of Moses hitting the rock with his staff. Moses was not obedient in this case, but the water still gushed forth. With that stated it wasn't the hitting of the rock that God was rebuking rather it was the words with which Moses spoke.

> **9** So Moses did as he was told. He took the staff from the place where it was kept before the Lord. **10** Then he and Aaron summoned the people to come and gather at the rock. "Listen, you rebels!" he shouted. "Must we bring you water from this rock?" **11** Then Moses raised his hand and struck the rock twice with the staff, and water gushed out. So the entire community and their livestock drank their fill. **12** But the Lord said to Moses and Aaron, "Because you did not trust me enough to demonstrate my holiness to the

> people of Israel, you will not lead them into the land I am giving them!" (Numbers 20:9-12, NLT)

It was because of Moses's words rebuking the children of Israel that God stated they did not trust the Lord to show his holiness to the people. Nevertheless, water still flowed from the rock. There are more cases when the one calling for the supernatural was not operating with God's blessing. Let's look at Peter, oh bless that great apostle. Yet, as great as he was; he still rushed in and blundered at times.

Just as a reminder, let's look at two obvious blunders. The first was the Apostle Paul having to openly rebuke Peter three times for showing prejudice against the gentile converts just to impress the Jewish converts. He didn't do this just one time but in at least three instances. Then we have the garden when Peter grabbed the sword and cut off the servant's ear. It was this same Peter who declared death over Ananias and Sapphira. Notice scripture does not say the Holy Spirit took their life. Rather, they dropped down dead.

> **5** As soon as Ananias heard these words, he fell to the floor and died. Everyone who heard about it was terrified. **6** Then some young men got up, wrapped him in a sheet, and took him out and buried him. (Acts 5:5-6, NLT)

I know many of you won't be convinced by this, so let's look at two other circumstances with the disciples wanting to call fire down from heaven. Jesus' response was, *"**56** For the Son of man is not come to destroy men's lives, but to save them. And they went to another village (Luke 9:56, KJV)."*

Then let's look at another incident of blasphemy of the Holy Spirit, that Peter was accusing them of:

> **31** Wherefore I say unto you, All manner of sin and blasphemy shall be forgiven unto men: but the blasphemy against the Holy Ghost shall not be forgiven unto men. **32** And whosoever speaketh a word against the Son of man, it shall be forgiven him: but whosoever speaketh against the Holy Ghost, it shall not be forgiven him, neither in this world, neither in the world to come. (Matthew 12:31-32, KJV)

The judgment against the Pharisees did not include a physical death. Peter was accusing Ananias and Sapphira of lying to the Holy Spirit which is blasphemy. Yet, when Jesus pronounced the Pharisees judgment, it did not include a physical death and the Pharisees sin was far greater than Ananias or his wife's. In fact, Sapphira at least spoke truthfully when questioned by Peter, while the Pharisees never repented of their accusations. Not to mention Jesus stating that he did not come to destroy men's lives, but to save them. God is no respecter of persons and doesn't discriminate in any way. Therefore, if indeed Peter's actions were correct, then the Pharisees should have immediately dropped dead as well. With all of this stated, there is only one conclusion that can be made: Peter acted outside the will of God on this matter. Yet, they still came to a supernatural ending.

Oh, yes, I know that this may totally mess with common theology, but then again, truth always contradicts the wisdom of men and their traditions.

The goal of this chapter is to show you how powerful the physical authority of men is, whether it is good or evil. I am pushing the boundaries of your knowledge of the supernatural. So, when it comes to talking about the authority we have In Christ, when we are walking in truth, you will see how limitless our authority is. Then, you will see yourself healed and healing others will be a cake walk. Let me show you through a less miraculous way that God shows us how in this physical world things are granted to us that are definitely not within his will.

The children of Israel, saw how other nations had kings. They wanted a king of their own. This was in direct opposition to God's will, yet they were accommodated by God:

> **4** Finally, all the elders of Israel met at Ramah to discuss the matter with Samuel. **5** "Look," they told him, "you are now old, and your sons are not like you. Give us a king to judge us like all the other nations have." **6** Samuel was displeased with their request and went to the Lord for guidance. **7** "Do everything they say to you," the Lord replied, "for they are rejecting me, not you. They don't want me to be their king any longer. **8** Ever since I brought them from Egypt they have continually abandoned me and followed other gods. And now they are giving you the same treatment. **9** Do as they ask, but solemnly warn them about the way a king will reign over them." (1 Samuel 8:4-9, NLT)

The most harmful religious teaching in all of creation is that God is in control. This teaching causes those who are serving God to lay down and just wait on God. Meanwhile, God is saying, "Use the authority I gave you!" just as He did with Moses at the Red Sea and with the disciples on the boat during the storm. God is sovereign as the dictionary definition defines sovereignty, but He does not take control and force His will on anyone.

> **Sovereignty** is the full right and power of a governing body over itself, without any interference from outside sources or bodies. One can also refer to a monarch who reigns over a sovereign realm as a sovereign. (Wikipedia)

He allows His creation to have free will, and in fact, gave us full authority on the Earth. Why do you think that Jesus told the disciples to pray thy kingdom come, thy will be done on Earth as it is in Heaven?

> **9** Pray like this: Our Father in heaven, may your name be kept holy. **10** May your Kingdom come soon. May your will be done on earth, as it is in heaven. (Matthew 6:9-10)

Does God retain ultimate power and authority? Of course, He does! But He also has structure and lets His creation make choices. Is His will always successfully obeyed on this Earth? No, it isn't. Therefore, Jesus taught His disciples to pray that God's Kingdom come and will be done, to get people to speak it out. That was before the cross. Now, His Kingdom has come, but we haven't seen the fullness of it yet because we're sitting on our hands and not using the authority, He gave us. Let's look into the unseen world for even more concrete proof that God gave mankind power over the world.

This is my paraphrase from the book of Enoch and covers most of chapters six through ten in that book: There were two hundred angels that were conspiring against mankind. Since they had no direct power over mankind they conspired to mate with women of the Earth. Thus, were the Nephilim born, they were part angel and part human.

These two hundred angels made the choice to disobey God. Which goes to show that God gives his creations the freedom to control their own lives. He had given angelic beings freedom to choose to disobey him. This totally disproves the notion that God controls all things. Is He ultimately in control? Yes, but He gives the freedom of choice. This totally disproves the "religious" definition of the sovereignty of God. We cannot point to everything that happens on this earth and blame God for it. Even angelic beings had the choice to mate with humans. They knew that they would be punished and severely so, which is why these two hundred angels made a pact with each other to carry out their plan.

> **3** And Semjaza, who was their leader, said unto them: I fear ye will not indeed agree to do this deed, and I alone shall have to pay the penalty of a great sin. **4** And they all answered him and said: Let us all swear an oath, and all bind ourselves by mutual imprecations not to abandon this plan but to do this thing." (Enoch 6:3-4)

Now, I'm going to digress just a bit. The names of their leaders were Semjazaz, Arakiba, Rameel, Kokabiel, Tamiel, Ramiel, Danel, Ezeqeel, Baraqijal, Asael, Armaros, Batarel, Ananel, Zaqiel, Samsapeel, Satarel, Turel, Jomjael, and Sariel. There wasn't one being named the Devil, Satan or Lucifer. Let me digress further. The book of Enoch even reveals the name of the angel that deceived Eve and the name was Gadreel, not The Devil, Satan, or Lucifer. Keep in mind all these watcher angels are bound forever.

> **6** And I remind you of the angels who did not stay within the limits of authority God gave them but left the place where they belonged. God has kept them securely chained in prisons of darkness, waiting for the great day of judgment. (Jude 1:6, NLT)

> 4 For God did not spare even the angels who sinned. He threw them into hell, in gloomy pits of darkness, where they are being held until the day of judgment. (2 Peter 2:4, NLT)

Notice, all of these watcher angels are bound. But here is the key: in order to access physical authority over the earth, there had to be flesh and blood. This was accomplished through the Nephilim. Before then, the watcher angels were merely observers and messengers. There was a heavenly council, but they were to speak to God on behalf of the human race. God stated to Enoch, *"And go, say to the Watchers of heaven, who have sent thee to intercede for them: You should intercede for men, and not men for you:" (Enoch 15:2)*

Notice that the watcher angels accessed human authority through taking human form, thus, desecrating themselves in the process.

God, the Heavenly Father, did no such thing when He formed Jesus. The Holy Spirit came upon Mary, which is how she conceived our Messiah. Therefore, Jesus referred to himself as both the Son of Man and the Son of God, in order to halt the corruption of the watcher angels. A greater one had to be born.

This really leads us to the next chapter and examining where human wisdom as we know it today, comes from. Recognizing the difference between human wisdom and God's Wisdom is paramount when wanting to walk as Jesus did, walking in the supernatural with God's Wisdom at all times. We take so much for granted as human beings that we completely miss out on how we were created to walk. What we see as sound, logical thinking is actually rationalization leading us into the trap of relying on the physical nature of things, not on the many blessings of Grace that Jesus provided for us.

Worksheet: Chapter 3

1. Describe what is meant by physical authority.

____

____

____

____

2. What is the one unforgivable sin? Give an example.

____

____

____

____

3. Do all miracles have to be directed originally by God? Why or why not?

____

____

____

____

4. What is the name of the angel that tempted Eve?

____

____

____

____

5. Other than the supernatural events listed in this chapter, name a different one that God didn't ordain but happened.

6. How did the angels' access physical authority?

7. With the information you've learned in your lifetime, where do you think man's knowledge came from? (to be answered in the next chapter)

8. What is the flavor I put in my latte'? 😊

NOTES:

4. The birthplace of Man's Wisdom

There may be many that feel that the last chapter about man's authority isn't true. Yet, all throughout scriptures are warnings about the words we speak. Whether you're a Christian or not, you have a huge amount of authority on this Earth. That really is undeniable. In my book, "Knocking Food Off Its Pedestal," there's over thirteen scriptures in there on our words. They have the power of life and death. Yet, all except a few people feel they are helpless, especially believers In Christ.

We become subject to food, diseases, germs, phobias, and the weather. We feel as if nearly everything has more power on this Earth than people. And, Lord have mercy, that doesn't even include "the devil," fallen angels and, God forbid, demons. Which is why the last topic, physical authority is so crucial to understand.

Many people would say: "Oh Tony, we've been given power over demons." If you really believed that then there would be no problem. Yet, believers are forever declaring the devil is after me, his demons are hounding me. Once you accept Christ, there is a target on your back and all the demons in hell are out to get you! C'mon people! In order to get the Truth that we are not simply pawns in the grand scheme of things and that the supernatural should abound in our lives, let's take a look at the wisdom of men.

We as a human race are trying to be problem solvers instead of being the solution. We look at a physical problem and feel like the solution has to be a physical solution. So then, we look to natural substances as the solution instead of looking to the Holy Spirit.

Where did this all start, us as physical beings relying on the physical nature of things? Yes, the first response would be when Adam ate the fruit. Shame hit Adam and Eve and they grabbed a physical substance to cover themselves up, the fig leaf. We know that. Let's dig deeper. But first, let's take a moment and enjoy a steaming cup of coffee! I start my mornings off with an americano, with a double espresso shot.

We've talked about how the rebellious angels needed flesh and blood in order to have authority over the Earth. What wasn't mentioned before was that the angels shared the secrets of heaven with their sons and daughters, the Nephilim. These secrets were all about what we consider things derived from natural resources. To quote from the book of Enoch, ***6*** *"Thou seest what Azazel hath done, who hath taught all unrighteousness on earth and revealed the eternal secrets which were (preserved in heaven), which men were striving to learn (Enoch, 9:6)."*

Let's take a look at this. Azazel was the angel that gave out the secrets of the metals of the Earth and taught us how to make the weapons of war. These were knives, shields, & breastplates. He also taught the art of making bracelets, ornaments, antimony, the secrets of the costly stones, coloring tinctures, and how to produce make-up.

It was Baraqijal, who taught astrology, Kokabel the constellations, Ezeqeel the knowledge of the clouds, Araqiel the signs of the Earth, Shamsiel the signs of the sun, and Sariel the course of the moon. Semjaza taught enchantments, root-cuttings, and made them acquainted with plants, and Armaros, the resolving of enchantments. These are just a few of the things that were taught. Penemue, taught the children of men the bitter and the sweet and instructed them in writing.

> **11** "For men were created exactly like the angels to the intent that they should continue pure and righteous, and death, which destroys everything could not have taken hold of them, but through this their knowledge they are perishing, and through this power it is consuming me." (Enoch 69:11)

Mankind was never to have known the use of the physical nature of things including writing. It was through the instruction of writing that all this knowledge was handed down from the Nephilim to all of mankind. Because there was a book written prior to the flood with all the knowledge that the angels had given their offspring, after the flood and when the Nephilim had been destroyed, it was a great grandson of Noah that found the book. Thus, this eternal knowledge continued. His name was Kainam, he found a writing carved in a rock and he sinned by writing it all down, because it was the teachings of the Watchers (Jubilees 8: 3-4). You might ask, "What is the point of all of this?" Everything that we consider as human knowledge that we think God showed mankind wasn't meant to be exposed to us at all. Plants, roots, the very foundation of medicine, was hidden from us. Why? Because we were created to rely on God for our every need. The angels taught their offspring for this purpose, to turn humankind away from relying (TRUSTING) on God to relying on the physical nature of things.

With all of that stated, I am not stating that the use of these things today is evil and wicked, for we do have freedom in Christ. But what we consider to be God given knowledge, isn't. It was purposed for evil by the angels and this knowledge was shared to their offspring.

I am not proposing to turn back time and destroy all these things, indeed, if that were even possible. But in order to truly understand the difference between Godly wisdom and the wisdom of men, we have to know the beginning of things. There is no condemnation in these things, but let's call a spade a spade. We were created to be supernatural, not subservient to the physical nature of things. How was the golden calf produced? By the knowledge given to us by the watcher angels. We as humans started worshiping the very things that were below us, subject to us, and we weren't even meant to have the knowledge about.

When I first started studying the book of Enoch and found out about writing with pen and paper, I thought to myself, "Phew! Good thing I use a laptop!" Then my thoughts turned to, "Okay! So, we now have knowledge that God never intended for us to have. Do I quit writing and stop using all of these things? Do I make my wife stop using make-up? What about my blue hair? Oh, my golly! I'm in sin!" We could take this information, really go insane, and create an extreme mess of things. I so praise Our Heavenly Father who knows all things and has given us His Holy Spirit to be able to walk in His wisdom!

> **28** And we know that God causes everything to work together for the good of those who love God and are called according to his purpose for them. (Romans 8:28, NLT)

Lord have mercy and thank you so much for this scripture and others like it. Even the knowledge that mankind was never supposed to have can be worked out for the good! The reason we're spending time on this is to show you what we consider to be God ordained wisdom and common knowledge, isn't. We were meant to live our lives sustained by Our Creator. Our lives were meant to be sustained by the supernatural.

> **8** Thine hand shall find out all thine enemies: thy right hand shall find out those that hate thee. **9** Thou shalt make them as a fiery oven in the time of thine anger: the Lord shall swallow them up in his wrath, and the fire shall devour them. **10** Their fruit shalt thou destroy from the earth, and their seed from among the children of men. **11** For they intended evil against thee: they imagined a mischievous device, which they are not able to perform. **12** Therefore shalt thou make them turn their back, when thou shalt make ready thine arrows upon thy strings against the face of them. **13** Be thou exalted, Lord, in thine own strength: so will we sing and praise thy power. (Psalm 21:8-13, KJV)

This scripture is talking about the Nephilim. David, himself went up against the seed of the Nephilim, remember Goliath? Throughout the Old Testament there were battles with the Nephilim. What we don't realize is that the God endorsed fighting and killing in the Old Covenant was against the corrupted seed of the watcher angels. Sodom and Gomorrah were destroyed for the same reason. Right there is the key to what God despises, the corrupted seed of man.

When scriptures are referring to the corrupted seed, that is the reference. We aren't talking about pure blood of man, but the corrupted seed of the watcher angels. That is where God's harshness is directed. How did the lineage of the Nephilim continue after the flood? There could have been three other uprisings from the watcher angels. The book of Enoch indicates that possibility. I personally lean toward the lineage continued through genetics by the wives of the sons of Noah. I'm digressing a bit here, but since that was brought up, let me prove that the lineage of the Nephilim, did continue after the flood. There are over thirty-three scriptures showing that the Nephilim still existed after the flood. Below are just a few of them.

> **33** And there we saw the giants, the sons of Anak, which come of the giants: and we were in our own sight as grasshoppers, and so we were in their sight. (Numbers 13:33, KJV)
>
> **20** (That also was accounted a land of giants: giants dwelt therein in old time; and the Ammonites call them Zamzummims; **21** A people great, and many, and tall, as the Anakims; but the Lord destroyed them before them; and they succeeded them, and dwelt in their stead: (Deuteronomy 2:20-21, KJV)
>
> **11** For only Og king of Bashan remained of the remnant of giants; behold his bedstead was a bedstead of iron; is it not in Rabbath of the children of Ammon? nine cubits was the length thereof, and four cubits the breadth of it, after the cubit of a man. (Deuteronomy 3:11, KJV)
>
> **12** All the kingdom of Og in Bashan, which reigned in Ashtaroth and in Edrei, who remained of the remnant of the giants: for these did Moses smite, and cast them out. (Joshua 13:12, KJV)
>
> **17** And there went out a champion out of the camp of the Philistines, named Goliath, of Gath, whose height was six cubits and a span. (1 Samuel 17:4, KJV)

> **16** And Ishbibenob, which was of the sons of the giant, the weight of whose spear weighed three hundred shekels of brass in weight, he being girded with a new sword, thought to have slain David. (2 Samuel 21:16, KJV)

> **20** And there was yet a battle in Gath, where was a man of great stature, that had on every hand six fingers, and on every foot six toes, four and twenty in number; and he also was born to the giant. (2 Samuel 21:20, KJV)

> **6** And yet again there was war at Gath, where was a man of great stature, whose fingers and toes were four and twenty, six on each hand, and six on each foot and he also was the son of the giant. (1 Chronicles 20:6, KJV)

A lot more instances than what you thought, right?

> **25** Who changed the truth of God into a lie, and worshipped and served the creature more than the Creator, who is blessed for ever. Amen. **26** For this cause God gave them up unto vile affections: for even their women did change the natural use into that which is against nature: **27** And likewise also the men, leaving the natural use of the woman, burned in their lust one toward another; men with men working that which is unseemly, and receiving in themselves that recompence of their error which was meet.**28** And even as they did not like to retain God in their knowledge, God gave them over to a reprobate mind, to do those things which are not convenient; **29** Being filled with all unrighteousness, fornication, wickedness, covetousness, maliciousness; full of envy, murder, debate, deceit, malignity; whisperers, **30** Backbiters, haters of God, despiteful, proud, boasters, inventors of evil things, disobedient to parents, **31** Without understanding, covenant breakers, without natural affection, implacable, unmerciful: **32** Who knowing the

> judgment of God, that they which commit such things are worthy of death, not only do the same, but have pleasure in them that do them. (Romans 1:25-32, KJV)

I believe that in the scriptures above, Paul is actually referencing the Nephilim. One of the reasons is that a reprobate mind is unrecoverable (so Paul cannot be referencing all Gentiles as is the common thought). There are no further chances. The Lord is so gracious and merciful to all, with the exception of the corrupted Nephilim seed and those that blasphemed the Holy Spirit because they had intimate knowledge of God. That is just food for thought. Yet, all of this is brought up for a purpose: to show how the secrets of heaven that weren't meant for mankind became human wisdom. Take a deep breath and ask the Holy Spirit if this is truth.

All of this was meant to throw us off from relying on God's Wisdom to relying on the wisdom of man. Yes, it is a shocker. But once you start to realize where the wisdom of man came from, it is easier to spot, root out of your life, and learn how to rely on the Holy Spirit in all things. When we learn that, then we can flow in the supernatural things of God as sons and start walking out life the way God ordained us to be. Now, we'll take a look at how severely God looked upon the sin of the angels and their offspring.

Let's set the stage for this. The whole world had turned corrupt. The souls of men who had been devoured by the Nephilim had cried out to the angels Michael, Gabriel, Uriel and Raphael who then took their petition to God. God then commanded that all sin be ascribed to Azazel, because of the works that he had corrupted mankind with. Now remember, Azazel was the watcher angel who taught the weapons of war, the use of metals, the single most destructive things. He ordered Azazel to be bound hand and foot and to be cast into darkness till the day of judgment and to cover his face in darkness. Then in the day of judgment, he shall be cast into the fire. The one who was ascribed all sin is already bound, never to be released. And his name wasn't the devil, Satan or Lucifer (that's another book). It was Azazel.

God did not stop there. He ordered Semijaza and all his associates to be bound till the day of judgment which would be in seventy generations. In those days, they shall be led to the abyss of fire to be held forever. God dealt quickly with them. He did not delay. Now, Enoch was asked by the watcher angels to take a petition for redemption before God Almighty. To which God responded.

> **4** Enoch thou scribe of righteousness, go, declare to the watchers of the heaven who have left the high heaven, the holy eternal place, and have defiled themselves with women, and have done as the children of earth do, and have taken unto themselves wives. **5** Ye have wrought great destruction on the earth. And ye shall have no peace nor forgiveness of sin: **6** and inasmuch as they delight themselves in their children The murder of their beloved ones shall they see and over the destruction of their children shall they lament, and shall make supplication unto eternity, but mercy and peace ye shall not attain." (Enoch 12:4-6)

> **12** Unto whom it was revealed, that not unto themselves, but unto us they did minister the things, which are now reported unto you by them that have preached the gospel unto you with the Holy Ghost sent down from heaven; which things the angels desire to look into. (1 Peter 1:12, KJV)

Based upon the book of Enoch, which things the angels desired to have, I believe would be more accurate. Notice how these angels have no hope for forgiveness of sin. The gospel is only set before mankind. Rather God's wrath is against the watcher angels that caused and taught mankind sin and against their offspring. The watcher angels saw the murder of their children in the flood. The flood wasn't sent to destroy those of pure blood, rather it was sent to destroy the Nephilim. Now, let's take a look at the sentence placed on the Nephilim.

> **9** And to Gabriel said the lord: Proceed against the bastards and the reprobates, and against the children of fornication: and destroy the children of fornication and the children of the Watchers from amongst men and cause them to go forth send them one against the other that they may destroy each other in battle: for length of days shall they not have. **10** And no request that they (ie. their fathers) make of thee shall be granted unto their fathers on their behalf; for they hope to live an eternal life, and each one of them will live five hundred years. (Enoch 10:9-10)

> **15** And destroy all the spirits of the reprobate and the children of the Watchers, because they have wronged mankind. **16** Destroy all wrong from the face of the earth and let every evil work come to an end: and let the plant of righteousness and truth appear… (Enoch 10:15-16)

Notice, "…destroy all the spirits of the reprobate." These would be the demons birthed from the dead Nephilim. What I want you to get is that God's judgment and harshness is against those who introduced the evils upon the Earth and to their offspring. This is the seed of corruption, or the corrupted seed. Often, that is referenced. But to the children of men, the loving Father is merciful, long suffering (extra patient), and it endures forever to those that accept Christ who is the pureness that came down from heaven.

Wow! That there is really a ton of information that most people are totally unaware of. If taken from the proper perspective, it will show why The Loving Father appears to be harsh and unforgiving in the Old Testament. That harshness wasn't against the children of men, but rather against the seed of corruption sown by the watcher angels. I would even go so far as to say that many times, even the men of God mistook His harshness and directed it towards the children of men not stained by the angels' seed. Remember, they had not received the revelations that we have today, nor did they have the Holy Spirit residing in them (or the One who is the true image of the Father, Christ Jesus). That is one of the two biggest points to be gleaned from this chapter.

The other point is that the secret knowledge stored up in the heavens was those things that we now think of as common knowledge. This common knowledge distracts us from having our true heritage. Trusting in those things is what creates a dam within ourselves causing the supernatural things of God to be halted, just like a dam blocks water from flowing. It disrupts our ability to see supernatural provision at work in our lives. Put the wisdom and knowledge of man in the right perspective, then the miracles will flow out of you like a raging river. This is our true heritage in Christ.

Worksheet: Chapter 4

1. Who was the watcher angel that deceived Eve? Hint: It isn't Satan, Lucifer, or the Devil?

2. Name five things that we look at as common that were actually the secrets things of heaven.

3. To whom was all sin ascribed to?

4. What was the sentence given to the transgressing watcher angels? How quickly were they bound?

5. Can the watcher angels be forgiven of their transgressions? Why or why not?

___

___

___

___

6. Who is the plant of righteousness and truth?

___

___

___

___

7. The sin of fornication is on one hand obvious, but what would be another definition of the word fornication?

___

___

___

___

8. Based upon the above answer, why does the Heavenly Father hate fornication so much?

___

___

___

___

9. Name the biggest two revelations Tony wants you to have from this chapter.

___

___

____

____

10. Somewhat more subtle, what is another point that Tony alludes to that will be in an upcoming book? (hint: it has to do with Satan, Lucifer, and "the Devil")

____

____

____

____

5. Nephilim: The Corrupted Seed

The seed had been planted, the seeds of evil. Yet, the kingdom of darkness as people love to call it, had been crushed before it was formed. The one angel that all sin had been ascribed to (Azazel) was bound hand and foot, never to see the light of day until judgment. All of the other fallen angels were bound as well. God wasn't playing around, as people love to insinuate. I truly want you to consider this. God took action against these angels yet, left one to roam the Earth for thousands of years causing chaos. I think we need to get a new theology.

In the same stream of things, how is it that God bound up the angels, but then left demons behind to harass humans? Once again, that is foolishness. The Most High God was furious that the Watcher Angels corrupted the human seed, and as we discussed in the last chapter, those watcher angels were to watch helplessly as their offspring were done away with. Their offspring was destroyed first by the flood, which then gave birth to demons because the Nephilim were half angelic. They were bound to the earth to destroy the remaining seed of the Watcher Angels, not humans.

> **8** And now the giants, who are produced from the spirits and flesh, shall be called evil spirits upon the earth, and on the earth shall be their dwelling. **9** Evil spirits have proceeded from their bodies; because they are born from men, and from the holy Watchers is their beginning and primal origin; they shall be evil spirits on earth, and evil spirits shall they be called. **10** As for the spirits of heaven, in heaven shall be their dwelling, but as for the spirits of the earth which were born upon the earth, on the earth shall be their dwelling. **11** And the spirits of the giants afflict, oppress, destroy, attack, do battle, and work destruction on the earth, and cause trouble: they take no food, but nevertheless hunger and thirst, and cause offenses. **12** And these spirits shall rise up against the children of men and against the women, because they have proceeded from them. (Enoch 15:8-12)

This judgment was given so that the corrupted seed should be destroyed by each other. God was using the spirits of the Nephilim to destroy the remaining Nephilim seed. They were not to touch the pure human lineage of Noah.

> **9** And He sent His sword into their midst that each should slay his neighbor, and they to slay each other till they all fell by the sword and were destroyed from the earth. **10** And their fathers were witnesses of their destruction, and after this they were bound in the depths of the earth for ever, until the day of the great condemnation, when judgment is executed on all those who have corrupted their ways and their works before the Lord. (Jubilees 5:9-10)

Their fathers were witnesses of their destruction. This is just as God had ordained it through Enoch. He used the evil spirits for this reason. However, the evil spirits (demons) did not abide by this. They started after Noah's sons who were purely human. This is when Noah approached God and asked that all the demons be imprisoned. ***6*** *"And let them not have power over the sons of the righteous from henceforth, and forever more"* ***7*** *And the Lord our God bade us to bind all. (Jubilees 10:6-7).* Once again confusion reigns because of a lack of understanding of these things. Mastema then petitioned the Lord saying *"I shall not be able to execute the power of my will on the sons of men, for these are for corruption and astray before my judgment, for great is the wickedness of the sons of men." (Jubilees 10:8)* This is where God commanded a tenth part of them remain, and nine parts into the place of condemnation. They were placed under control of Mastema, and, get this, *"Thus the evil spirits were precluded from hurting the sons of Noah." (Jubilees 10:13)*

Mastema was to keep the ten percent of demons left to dwell on the earth in line. They were only to touch the corrupted seed. Remember that at this time, mankind had yet to receive the Holy Spirit, once again being prone to man's misperception and also to mistranslation. That is why I've added my two cents into the scenario.

Just as the demons had overstepped their boundaries by harassing the sons of Noah, they did the same after Noah's sons had passed. Suffice it to say that the tenth part that was left on the Earth were put into the pit upon the crucifixion of Jesus. The demons knew that with the coming of Jesus, their end was near, and their destruction was upon them. From Noah to Jesus, God did not just let people be at the demons' mercy. That was when He gave mankind the power to cast demons out. The demons never had unlimited power on the Earth. Their only power was lies that were believed. They were never to touch the children of Israel, yet they did.

These things had to be approached at least partially because as long as you think there is an outside force of resistance coming against you, then there is. There was a corruption and that corruption came from the watcher angels and their knowledge that was to be hidden from men. Jesus is the incorruptible seed. Therefore, evil which was born of the corruptible seed is now fully defeated. What we see happening on this earth is the result of what had been planted by the Watcher Angels. Jesus achieved total victory at the cross over a number of things. One of those things was the ten percent of the demons that were left on the Earth to destroy the corrupted seed. They were defeated and bound as well. The evil which were the watcher angels had long been bound. Then at the cross, the demons were then cast into bondage. Yes, I know for many of you that is a hard pill for you to swallow.

> **29** They began screaming at him, "Why are you interfering with us, Son of God? Have you come here to torture us before God's appointed time?" (Mathew 8:29, NLT)
>
> **34** "Go away! Why are you interfering with us, Jesus of Nazareth? Have you come to destroy us? I know who you are—the Holy One of God!" (Luke 4:34, NLT)
>
> **24** "Why are you interfering with us, Jesus of Nazareth? Have you come to destroy us? I know who you are—the Holy One of God!" (Mark 1:24, NLT)

These are curious questions. "Why are you interfering with us, Son of God? Have you come to destroy us?" They knew who Jesus was and they also knew His coming signified that their end was at hand. There was a designated time for their end all because they were of the corrupted seed of the watcher angels. The end of the age was when their end was to come. And that end of the age happened with the fulfillment of the Old Covenant in Christ.

There are no more demons as in the spirits of the Nephilim. I know that raises up a whole lot of questions such as what about the book of Acts? All of this gets into an entirely different area of discussion, which is the exact time of the end of the age. That discussion, because of what is taught in mainstream Christianity, is an entirely different book. "Ok, Tony. So, you're dodging that question. What about this experience I had or that experience? And then, if all of that is truly done away with, why is there still evil in the world? The answer is simple: from the evil imaginations of the heart. This explanation ties in with all the previous chapters.

Flesh and blood were given the authority on the Earth. When a lie is believed and spoken either with spoken words or the empowerment of heart beliefs, it happens on this earth. Just take a look at the movies created about demons, the Devil, the fallen angels. Let's take it even further back.

The Jews and even the gentiles who were alive during the days of Christ knew about demons as they were originally. To the Jews who didn't accept Christ, in their minds, demons still wandered around because the Messiah hadn't come yet. The converted Jews had trouble with transitioning from the Law of Moses to Christianity. The carryover result was that they believed in their minds that demons were still roaming the earth. So therefore, they still had the power to harass people.

The memories of these demons were still being handed down by tradition. If a person believes that something exists, then it does. Imagine an entire generation that believed they (demons) still existed. This is why many still give power to entities that had long since been bound and imprisoned. Right now, we're just talking about Jews and Christians. Throw into the pot the pagan beliefs on spiritual powers. Repeating the question then why does it appear that Jesus did nothing about them? Because mankind as a majority still believes they exist.

Spells, incantations, and all other appearances of evil still happen because we believe that they are drawing their power from these evil spiritual authorities when in fact they are using the physical authority of humankind. And where did that knowledge come from? The watcher angels giving the eternal secrets to mankind, the secrets we were never meant to know. From every side of the spectrum demons are believed to still be functioning. So, it's no small surprise it falsely appears as if they are. Christians magnify them in their fighting "spiritual warfare." In the pulpits, the powers of demons and "satans" are magnified. Those who aren't Christians magnify them as stated before, in movies and television shows. You ever heard of Halloween? Yet, we wonder why they appear to be real. It's called vain imagination, folks.

In scriptures we are warned of the power of the tongue, our words. Yet, we keep pronouncing and declaring the powers of the "devil," demons, and spiritual principalities. Who is then creating the evil? Yes, mankind is. In fact, we make them up and give them names, and when you name something, you give it life. Jezebel is an excellent example of this. In scriptures she is never mentioned as being a demon or a spirit. Yet, ministers have created her to be a principality.

> **20** "But I have this complaint against you. You are permitting that woman—that Jezebel who calls herself a prophet—to lead my servants astray. She teaches them to commit sexual sin and to eat food offered to idols. (Revelation 2:20, NLT)

Notice it states you are permitting that woman who calls herself a prophet. There isn't even an insinuation that she was ever anything more, principality or demon. This is talking about people that have the same mindset as Jezebel had, nothing more. Then, we turn around and glamorize a woman that's been dead for over two thousand years and give her power and authority she never had. She was so powerful that she ended up being eaten by dogs. I say that with all the sarcasm that I can mustard up.

> **32** Jehu looked up and saw her at the window and shouted, "Who is on my side?" And two or three eunuchs looked out at him. **33** "Throw her down!" Jehu yelled. So they threw her out the window, and her blood spattered against the wall and on the horses. And Jehu trampled her body under his horses' hooves. **34** Then Jehu went into the palace and ate and drank. Afterward he said, "Someone go and bury this cursed woman, for she is the daughter of a king." **35** But when they went out to bury her, they found only her skull, her feet, and her hands. **36** When they returned and told Jehu, he stated, "This fulfills the message from the Lord, which he spoke through his servant Elijah from Tishbe: 'At the plot of land in Jezreel, dogs will eat Jezebel's body. **37** Her remains will be scattered like dung on the plot of land in Jezreel, so that no one will be able to recognize her.'" (2 Kings 9:32-37, NLT)

Yet, we have made her into an immortal, all-powerful being. People make money writing books on how to break the power of Jezebel! That is really disgusting. It is no different than creating false gods.

This is what we've done with the whole evil spiritual side of things. We've made Christianity into a "spiritual warfare" that Jesus took care of. God vs Satan. There was never an angel that could stand up to God. That is why they are all bound in hell. And it isn't Christians vs. Satan either. We are meant to carry the message of salvation which absolutely includes seeing people set free from every form of evil. Jesus already took care of the beings called demons. Now, we're fighting vain imagination that is keeping people bound and oppressed through our own natural authority.

Let's talk about the imagination. It's a powerful thing:

> **6** And the Lord said, Behold, the people is one, and they have all one language; and this they begin to do: and now nothing will be restrained from them, which they have imagined to do. (Genesis 11:6, KJV)
>
> **3** This is what the Sovereign Lord says: What sorrow awaits the false prophets who are following their own imaginations and have seen nothing at all!' (Ezekiel 13:3, NLT)
>
> **17** "Now, son of man, speak out against the women who prophesy from their own imaginations. (Ezekiel 13:17, NLT)
>
> **5** Casting down imaginations, and every high thing that exalteth itself against the knowledge of God, and bringing into captivity every thought to the obedience of Christ; (2 Corinthians 10:5, KJV)

A thing is conceived in the heart, then happens. Once again, this is human authority. And nothing will be impossible for them. Of course, this is with the wrong use of our imagination. Yet, this speaks of the power and authority that comes about through our imagination. "Casting down imaginations and every high thing that exalteth itself against the knowledge of God."

So, a thought that God who is our Father would allow a spiritual being to harass His children is a high thing that exalts itself against the knowledge of Christ. Thinking that a satan could go against God's Will is another thought that is exalting itself against God. The Father doesn't make robots. Angels are obviously given free will as well. The exception is that they aren't given a second chance because of their direct knowledge and experience with God and the heavens. They have no option of the gospel.

Here's another food for thought: Jesus was given all power and authority and appointed King and High Priest. Yet, there are supposed spiritual principalities and powers over regions that control cities. If that isn't a thought that exalts itself against the knowledge of God, then I don't know what is. In the entire book of Acts there is not one statement indicating that Paul ever bound the "spiritual" authority over a city. Peter in his address on the day of Pentecost he never even spoke of a devil, demon, or spiritual being that was trying to stop them from believing. Who was it that tried to stop the message of the Gospel from spreading? Other men, the religious leaders.

> **23** As soon as they were freed, Peter and John returned to the other believers and told them what the leading priests and elders had said. **24** When they heard the report, all the believers lifted their voices together in prayer to God: "O Sovereign Lord, Creator of heaven and earth, the sea, and everything in them— **25** you spoke long ago by the Holy Spirit through our ancestor David, your servant, saying, 'Why were the nations so angry? Why did they waste their time with futile plans? **26** The kings of the earth prepared for battle; the rulers gathered together against the Lord and against his Messiah. **27** "In fact, this has happened here in this very city! For Herod Antipas, Pontius Pilate the governor, the Gentiles, and the people of Israel were all united against Jesus, your holy servant, whom you anointed. **28** But everything they did was determined beforehand according to your will. **29** And now, O Lord, hear their threats, and give us, your servants, great boldness in preaching your word. **30** Stretch out your hand with healing

> power; may miraculous signs and wonders be done through the name of your holy servant Jesus." **31** After this prayer, the meeting place shook, and they were all filled with the Holy Spirit. Then they preached the word of God with boldness. (Acts 4:23-31, NLT)

Where are the opposing forces of demons and fallen angels? Not mentioned at all, that's where. Whenever we think there is unseen resistance, it is created by our beliefs. The apostles never fell for it. You see, in the above verses Peter mentions the prophesy of David in which he only mentions the kings of the earth, the rulers gathered together against the LORD, and his Messiah. Then Peter goes on and states that it was fulfilled right there in this very city, and he mentions names. All were earthly people. Herod, Pontius Pilate, the Gentiles and the people of Israel. Where are the hordes of demons? Where is the binding of Satan, as is the custom today? The satans were already bound. That's why there is no mention of them. The truth of the matter is that when we put down these vain imaginations and start spreading the Good News of Christ, then we will see the supernatural and people coming to Jesus in droves.

Most Christians are right aside Satanists in boldly declaring how powerful the Devil is. There is only one power in the heavens and on the Earth, and that is the Heavenly Father who has given all power and authority to Christ Jesus.

> **18** Jesus came and told his disciples, "I have been given all authority in heaven and on earth. **19** Therefore, go and make disciples of all the nations, baptizing them in the name of the Father and the Son and the Holy Spirit. **20** Teach these new disciples to obey all the commands I have given you. And be sure of this: I am with you always, even to the end of the age." (Matthew 28:18-20, NLT)

The common teaching that Jesus has all authority and that the devil has no authority but has ability is balderdash. The reason why there is still evil committed on the face of this Earth is because of choices made by humans. We are not yet in God's Rest because we are fighting the wrong battle. Instead of coming to the truth by the renewing of the mind we are fighting an evil kingdom that appears to be more powerful than Christ. My best example of this is: ***10*** *The thief's purpose is to steal and kill and destroy. My purpose is to give them a rich and satisfying life. (John 10:10, NLT)*

If you are asked to write down who the thief is, ninety eight percent of you will write down the Devil, Satan, or Lucifer. What'd you write down or think in the last worksheet? Yup! That proves my point. Jesus references who the thief is and it's a person, not a spiritual being.

> **1** "I tell you the truth, anyone who sneaks over the wall of a sheepfold, rather than going through the gate, must surely be a thief and a robber!... 8 All who came before me were thieves and robbers. But the true sheep did not listen to them. (John 10:1,8, NLT)

Jesus was specifically talking about those who would not recognize him for who He was, namely the Pharisees, Saducees and the other religious authorities. These were flesh and blood, not spiritual beings. For those that are not convinced "All who came before me." He was speaking as a man to men because as a spiritual being, **none came before Him.** Demons recognized Jesus and feared Him. The religious leaders did not. Therefore, this is in reference to men and not to demons, Satan, the Devil or Lucifer.

Worksheet: Chapter 5

1. Who was given all the authority in the heavens and on the Earth? So, do demons have any authority over us?

____
____
____
____

2. What was the sentence for the evil spirits? This is a two-part answer.

____
____
____
____

3. Is Jezebel a spirit? If you answer yes, prove it with scriptures.

____
____
____
____

4. Who is the thief in John 10:10?

____
____
____
____

5. Who were united against Jesus according to Peter, and when did that happen?

____
____
____
____

6. Define 'casting down imaginations and everything that exalts itself above God.'

____
____
____
____

NOTES:

____
____
____
____

6. Jesus Mentoring his Brothers

We're switching gears, but for those who were overwhelmed by the last chapter, let's look at my healing. Here was a former atheist who hadn't even read scriptures, was suicidal, had severe PTSD, angry, and literally couldn't be accused of being sane. Yet, I was healed without someone else "doing deliverance." In other words, no one had to yell and scream at "the Devil," or even offer a two- or three-hour interview for repenting of all my past sins. It was evident that in most Pentecostal eyes, I would've had hundreds of demons. Being an entirely brand-new believer, I would've been chopped liver for "the devil" or demons.

Yet, in just a few minutes I was completely set free with no idea of the popular ways of deliverance. It is the Love of Christ and freedom in the truth that sets people free. Our warfare isn't against flesh and blood. This is true. It is, however, against vain imagination and thoughts that exalts themselves over the

Knowledge of God. Let's now enjoy a moment of relaxation with a hot americano.

Imagination can be used for the cause of getting beliefs submitted into our hearts. Imagine this, a baby from planet Krypton comes down from the sky. He grows up and does many supernatural things, saves people, helps people and rights many wrongs. Who doesn't love Superman? What if Superman states that you can become exactly like him? Would you jump at that opportunity or would you hem and haw in unbelief? Got some news for you. More than likely you have already hem and hawed in unbelief.

We've had the Son of God come down from heaven, turn water into wine, feed thousands of people with just a few fish and a couple loaves of bread, retrieve a gold coin from a fish's mouth, walk on water, calm storms, and then He states: greater things than these shall you do. Yet, we rationalize this away and we don't believe it, all the while believing that evil people using evil spirits can cast spells, cause storms, curse people, send people diseases, and do other incredibly evil things. Does anyone else see this as insanity?

Then the flip side of the coin is accusing God, who sent the Son to do only good, of causing this stuff to happen or sitting lazily by and watching it all happen under the guise that, "He's got His reasons." That's insanity!

Or, how about this? We believe that unseen beings can just enter a person and cause them to do wrong. Yet, being supernaturally healed is a myth and impossible. We think that by touching inanimate objects people can go insane. Yet, it is insane to believe that food can supernaturally multiply. Or we believe in one evil spiritual being that can make tires go flat, cause the loss of a job, cause adultery, and all the things that go wrong in life (for millions of people all over the world at the same time). That would be the very definition of insanity, all while declaring that God is our heavenly Father.

Meanwhile, the Son of God is showing his disciples what is possible and having them do the same things that He did.

> **12** "I tell you the truth, anyone who believes in me will do the same works I have done, and even greater works, because I am going to be with the Father. (John 14:12, NLT)

Anyone who believes in me will do the same works I have done. So, the greater works isn't just getting on the internet and having church online. It's doing the same things and then even more. Let's look at it once again.

Jesus turned water into wine, multiplied food, walked on water, had money appear in a fish's mouth, calmed storms, translated from one spot to another, did that very thing with boats as well, not to mention the huge amount of healings, etc. He even proved that He meant everyone by appointing seventy other people.

These people aren't mentioned by name. They were just a random group of people. They weren't in Jesus' inner circle. Still, we think there has to be a title in order to see miracles and live in the supernatural. That, my dear friends, is not what Jesus showed us. In fact, there was a man casting out devils and the disciples told him to stop it. Jesus rebuked the disciples and told them to leave him and others like him alone. How much clearer can this be? Jesus hadn't appointed this man. That should really tell us something.

> **1** The Lord now chose seventy-two other disciples and sent them ahead in pairs to all the towns and places he planned to visit. (Luke 10:1, NLT)

> **38** John said to Jesus, "Teacher, we saw someone using your name to cast out demons, but we told him to stop because he wasn't in our group." **39** "Don't stop him!" Jesus said. "No one who performs a miracle in my name will soon be able to speak evil of me. (Mark 9:38-39, NLT)

Many of you already understand a lot of this which is why I'm not going to spend a lot of time trying to convince you of this. But for those of you who are super sensitive to the thought, "Well, we have to have a special word from God to do these things," let's take a look at the wedding: **4** "*Dear woman, that's not our problem," Jesus replied. "My time has not yet come." (John 2:4, NLT)*

One: This miracle was for such a frivolous thing such as people enjoying themselves and celebrating. Two: Jesus states it was before His time. Yet, He did it in spite of this. Now, it is common knowledge to us that Jesus did this. But it wasn't announced to anyone that He had done this. So, for those that think it was for a sign, or some special purpose, guess again. The only ones that knew were Mary, the disciples, and the servants. Jesus wasn't being theatrical about this like a magician doing a magic trick.

> **6** Standing nearby were six stone water jars, used for Jewish ceremonial washing. Each could hold twenty to thirty gallons. **7** Jesus told the servants, "Fill the jars with water." When the jars had been filled, **8** he said, "Now dip some out, and take it to the master of ceremonies." So the servants followed his instructions. **9** When the master of ceremonies tasted the water that was now wine, not knowing where it had come from (though, of course, the servants knew), he called the bridegroom over. **10** "A host always serves the best wine first," he said. "Then, when everyone has had a lot to drink, he brings out the less expensive wine. But you have kept the best until now!" (John 2:6-10, NLT)

Do you see how non-theatrical this was? In fact, scripture doesn't even state that the servants told anyone about it. All Jesus said was to fill the jars with water and take some to the master of ceremonies. This is just like with Jesus telling Peter to go to the river and get the coin out of the fish's mouth.

> **27** However, we don't want to offend them, so go down to the lake and throw in a line. Open the mouth of the first fish you catch, and you will find a large silver coin. Take it and pay the tax for both of us." (Matthew 17:27, NLT)

This, once again, wasn't a show-off magic trick. This was a conversation between Jesus and Peter. Peter wasn't running off at the mouth blabbing this to everyone. In fact, Jesus had him throw a line in for appearance sake. Once again, this was a need that was fulfilled without it being common knowledge. Through this, Jesus paid the taxes for both himself and Peter. There isn't even a scripture that states Peter ran off and told the other disciples. We can learn from this. The supernatural should be a part of our daily lives. Now, Jesus could have told Peter to go get Judas who was the treasurer and get him to pay the tax. He didn't. Here's another point: this was all before the Cross, before the Holy Spirit was poured out.

The game changer is this is long before we became sons of God and part of the Kingdom of God. Here's what we don't realize is that there are signs and wonders for the unbeliever. These things aren't meant to be signs and wonders for believers. They should be a part of the believer's daily walk.

After Jesus' resurrection when Jesus stated to lay hands on the sick and they shall recover, that was for the unbeliever. The believer has Divine Health because of the Holy Spirit in them. This is the hardest thing for people to grasp. We as believers don't need someone to lay hands on us. Laying on of hands was for the unbelievers. Okay. Okay. I'll prove it to you:

> **4** And because of his glory and excellence, he has given us great and precious promises. These are the promises that enable you to share his divine nature and escape the world's corruption caused by human desires. (2 Peter 1:4, NLT)

These are the promises that enable you to share his divine nature, you are sharing his divine nature. His divine nature is supernatural in all things which includes divine health and ALL needs. Was Jesus ever sick even before the Cross? Nope. Is he in heaven capable of being sick? No. Does Jesus in His Divine Nature have to use natural/physical means for anything? Nope. It's that very nature that we share. Let's go to the next scripture.

> **8** The more you grow like this, the more productive and useful you will be in your knowledge of our Lord Jesus Christ. 9 But those who fail to develop in this way are shortsighted or blind, forgetting that they have been cleansed from their old sins. (2 Peter 1:8-9, NLT)

Peter was talking to the Jews because he was sent to the Jews. So, in the part that he states forgetting that they have been cleansed from their old sins, he's including sickness. The Jews believed that sickness came about from sin. If they had been cleansed from their old sins, then they had been healed as well.

> **24** He personally carried our sins in his body on the cross so that we can be dead to sin and live for what is right. By his wounds you are healed." (1 Peter 2:24, NLT)

When reading the epistles of John, James and Peter, we forget they are writing to the Jews who had lived their whole lives under the Law of Moses. We then misinterpret what they are truly saying because the majority of us don't understand the culture. We read scriptures with a Western viewpoint, so we come to the wrong conclusions. All of the epistles are letters written to a specific group of people, for specific reasons. Unless you unbiasedly listen to the Holy Spirit and study to understand what the author is truly saying you will misunderstand and take the scriptures out of context.

> **17** Elijah was as human as we are, and yet when he prayed earnestly that no rain would fall, none fell for three and a half years! **18** Then, when he prayed again, the sky sent down rain and the earth began to yield its crops. (James 5:17-18, NLT)

This shows exactly what I'm saying. James was trying to show the converts that they all had unharnessed power. There are a few things that may throw some people off. First, is verse fourteen where it says to call for the elders of the church. From this, people get the assumption that only appointed leaders of the church can pray and cause things to happen. Let's take a look at the next verse which is for every single person.

> **16** Confess your sins to each other and pray for each other so that you may be healed. The earnest prayer of a righteous person has great power and produces wonderful results. (James 5:16, NLT)

James here is talking to every single person, not just to leadership. They are told to confess their sins to each other to clear their conscience. They were just learning the New Covenant and did not know their identity in Christ yet. These were Jews under the Law of Moses which had lived their own lives being judged "by their actions," not by Christ's action.

The word prayer also throws people off. They then start begging and pleading for God to do something and nothing happens because they doubt. As shown before with Joshua and the sun standing still, Joshua didn't beg or plead with God. He spoke out what he wanted to happen. The same with Elijah. He commanded the drought and later, the rain to come. Jesus always made a command statement, not a plea. The apostles never pled, they made command statements as well.

It is so wonderful that James uses the example of Elijah and the weather. Once again, he is trying to show the Jewish converts the power we have in Christ. It's not limited to simply healing the sick. We have this power in all areas of our lives. He starts off stating that Elijah was only a man as we are and then uses the example of him commanding the weather. The earnest prayer of a righteous person has great power and produces wonderful results. Who is righteous? We are In Christ.

Prayer is a command, not a plea, and it pertains to all of life. Notice how James says, "great power and wonderful results," and backs it up with an example of the prophet whose life was one of tremendous power, calling him just a man as we are! See the significance in these statements? Now we're getting to the heart of this chapter. Until now, you've been eased into this.

You are the very fabric of God. When we become believers, the Holy Spirit comes into us and there is no difference between us and Jesus. "What blasphemy, Tony!" Yet, when the true realization of what happens when we're reborn in the spirit sinks in, then nothing shall by any means harm us. We're reborn in the spirit and become supernatural beings because spirit is greater than the physical nature of things.

I've got to digress for a moment, cause there's a common thing that happens with believers who start realizing this truth. They start saying that Jesus was in the mall today and healed a person. This insinuates that the one who prayed over a person is Jesus. No, you're name ain't Jesus. My name isn't Jesus. My name is Tony and your name is your name. We carry His spirit and we are now sons of God, but we weren't the first born. Christ Jesus is the first born of many. He alone is the Messiah, Savior and King. My pet peeve is this insinuation can cause arrogance. That covers one side of the spectrum.

Then there's the side that states you're comparing yourself to Jesus. That it's blasphemous to do so. He's in me and that's the same reason why Jesus was crucified for comparing himself to God.

We have been living in a diluted state of Christianity. We've conformed to the foolishness of the world's wisdom, not God's wisdom. And this so much so that we call the wisdom of men God's wisdom. Why do we choose a certain diet then call it God's Wisdom? Does God need a physical substance to keep his children healthy? And if you eat the wrong physical substance, God who calls you his child can do nothing about it? We claim medicine comes from God when it didn't. It came from fallen angels. Does God need to spill blood (surgery) in order to heal? How about removing faulty organs? The loving Heavenly Father did such a poor job in creating us that He had to give knowledge to humans to cut into a person's body and remove defective organs. Really? Then we say, "No, God didn't create defective bodies. We haven't taken care of them which is why they break down." So then, God's creation is subject to physical substances? Is that really the truth?

The problem isn't the creator. The problem is we have substituted God's Wisdom for man's foolish wisdom. Did Jesus ever do surgery on a person? Or tell them what to eat to cure them? It is time to re-evaluate and decide what true, Godly wisdom looks like. Please don't be stupid. If you need surgery while learning the difference between Godly Wisdom and Man's Wisdom, get the surgery. Now, let's prove that we are sons of God right this moment on this earth.

> **14** For all who are led by the Spirit of God are children of God. (Romans 8:14, NLT)
>
> **18** And I will be your Father, and you will be my sons and daughters, says the Lord Almighty." (2 Corinthians 6:18, NLT)
>
> **1** See how very much our Father loves us, for he calls us his children, and that is what we are! But the people who belong to this world don't recognize that we are God's children because they don't know him. **2** Dear friends, we are already God's children, but he has not yet shown us what we will be like when Christ appears. But we do know that we will be like him, for we will see him as he really is. **3** And all who have this eager expectation will keep themselves pure, just as he is pure. (1 John 3:1-3, NLT)

We are already God's children. This was John who walked with Jesus' writing. John, who himself had seen the supernatural and performed the supernatural. John was the only one of the original twelve not to be martyred. What throws people off is John saying, "that he has not yet shown us what we will be like." Then, we sink back into thinking sometime in the future. So, for now we think we're still powerless mere mortals. This way of thinking just isn't true. That was two thousand years ago, in the early church.

Christ has been revealed to us, the Father is continually moving us forward. Each generation has leaders who God has given revelation for that specific generation. What was true in Moses' generation, was no longer true for John's generation. What was revealed to John didn't stay stagnant either. With each generation came more revelation.

> **18** So the Jewish leaders tried all the harder to find a way to kill him. For he not only broke the Sabbath, he called God

> his Father, thereby making himself equal with God. (John 5:18, NLT)

Why then do we think it is blasphemy to say that we are capable of all the things that Jesus did and more? Why is that such a hard thing to grasp?

> **6** I say, 'You are gods; you are all children of the Most High. (Psalm 82:6, NLT)

If we are gods, because we are children of the Most High, then why do we conform to this world and think that being poor, sick, diseased and broken is the normal?

> **32** "So don't be afraid, little flock. For it gives your Father great happiness to give you the Kingdom. (Luke 12:32, NLT)

Wait just one moment! Isn't the Kingdom of God supernatural? Therefore, in God's Kingdom the supernatural should be natural.

> **29** For God knew his people in advance, and he chose them to become like his Son, so that his Son would be the firstborn among many brothers and sisters. **30** And having chosen them, he called them to come to him. And having called them, he gave them right standing with himself. And having given them right standing, he gave them his glory. (Romans 8:29-30, NLT)

Are you telling me that we have God's Glory, living inside of us, then why are we fearful of anything?

> **49** And as we have borne the image of the earthy, we shall also bear the image of the heavenly. (1 Corinthians 15:49, KJV)

This is available for us right now when we believe this. Did not Enoch receive his heavenly body even before Jesus came? It wasn't because of a future mission. Scripture clearly states it was because of His faith pleasing God. And as Jesus is, so are we in this world!

> **11** So now Jesus and the ones he makes holy have the same Father. That is why Jesus is not ashamed to call them his brothers and sisters. (Hebrews 2:11, NLT)

If we are brothers and sisters, then we share the same traits. If we share the same traits, then the supernatural is natural and we have access to all truth now.

> **4** But when the right time came, God sent his Son, born of a woman, subject to the law. **5** God sent him to buy freedom for us who were slaves to the law, so that he could adopt us as his very own children. **6** And because we are his children, God has sent the Spirit of his Son into our hearts, prompting us to call out, "Abba, Father." **7** Now you are no longer a slave but God's own child. And since you are his child, God has made you his heir. (Galatians 4:4-7, NLT)

We are heirs, which means we have access to everything now.

> **13** This will continue until we all come to such unity in our faith and knowledge of God's Son that we will be mature in the Lord, measuring up to the full and complete standard of Christ. (Ephesians 4:13, NLT)

The full and complete standard of Christ. This includes the miracles Jesus performed, and much more. The Father never wanted his children to have need for money, nor dependence upon other men. There was only to be one King and one Kingdom. He never intended Israel to be subject to kings. How did that work out? Yet, he let them have their way. It is up to us to come to the fullness of who we are in Christ. It is our decision whether or not to access the full knowledge and faith of Jesus. Yet, we keep striving to lean on man's foolish wisdom and think it is more powerful than His Holy Spirit inside of us.

Most Christians are still waiting to die and go to heaven for a true, immortal experience when it is available to us now. We say nothing is impossible with God, but act like Him making us true sons and daughters with the power and authority of an heir is impossible. That is what it comes down to. We think that it's impossible for God to work through us to make the supernatural happen.

Worksheet: Chapter 6

1. Name three things that we believe is actually human wisdom, not God's.

____
____
____
____
____
____

2. Name seven things that you would love to see happen supernaturally that you thought would be impossible.

____
____
____
____
____
____

3. Define human wisdom.

____
____
____
____
____
____

4. Define God's Wisdom.

5. Describe what is our true nature as sons of God. Push the boundaries.

6. Name two miracles Jesus performed, that He did just because he could. Yup! I worded it that way just to provoke you.

7. Take a few minutes to imagine some small normal action that you do every day. Now, become supernatural imagining it in your mind. The sky's the limit! Describe it.

8. Take a few minutes to imagine a supernatural event that you can use to help someone else. Describe it.

Notes:

7. Born of the spirit, as a child of God

We are born of the Spirit. We've been reborn and now we are sons of God. A son takes on the traits of the father in this physical existence. Then, we take on the traits of our True Father when we are in Christ. We are no longer constrained by the physical limitations of the first Adam because we are now born into the second Adam, Jesus. We tend to say things like we are His sons and daughters. Yet, we deny our very nature. How is it that witchcraft working through us is more believable than The Father's power working through his sons and daughters? Let's take a moment to indulge ourselves in a hot cup of coffee and think about that.

There is no power in the way we view or say we are sons of God when we separate the spiritual from the natural. When we compartmentalize and divide the two as independent from each other, the spiritual things of God are somewhere out there in heaven, not in us. We're in God's Kingdom but helplessly look for a politician to save us. We say Jesus is our King but argue politics and are looking for a human savior (got news for you, he already came and his name is Jesus, not our president). We view earth as outside of heaven, not as a part of God's domain. We say we are the temple of the Holy Spirit, but that only applies as a means to threaten people into conforming to this world. You better eat the right things, show up at church on Sundays, exercise, and take care of the temple. Yet, if a bad circumstance happens, we run to a doctor, lawyer, or some other human. Who, by our actions, we are saying has more power to change our circumstance than the One who dwells within us.

> **17** By living in God, love has been brought to its full expression in us so that we may fearlessly face the day of judgment, because all that Jesus now is, so are we in this world. (1 John 4:17, TPT)

Notice all that Jesus now is, we are. Jesus is not fearful of sickness, witchcraft, or any other evil. He is in his glorious body. He isn't dependent on any physical substance nor is he living in any type of fear. Let this sink in. Love has been brought to its full expression in us. In other words, the Father's love for his sons will protect us, we are not subject to this world. It is subject to us. "Tony you better watch it. God shares his glory with no one." I beg to differ. We are one with him. We are no longer separate from him. Therefore, we are His glory.

> **21** I pray for them all to be joined together as one even as you and I, Father, are joined together as one. I pray for them to become one with us so that the world will recognize that you sent me. **22** For the very glory you have given to me I have given them so that they will be joined together as one and experience the same unity that we enjoy. **23** You live fully in me and now I live fully in them so that they will experience perfect unity, and the world will be convinced

> that you have sent me, for they will see that you love each one of them with the same passionate love that you have for me. (John 17: 21-23, TPT)

Do you see that we are God's Glory? If we are his glory, then nothing shall be impossible. We often have a false humility which diminishes the Holy Spirit's ability to work through us. Just as the sons of Jacob would loudly proclaim, "We are the sons of Jacob and will destroy your city," they had pride in their father and leaned on Jacob's favor with God. Now, we can proudly proclaim, "God is my father. So, I pour favor on you." We can now decree something to be done on the Earth and it will happen. In fact, that is what we are called to do.

If we are in perfect unity with the Father, Son, and Holy Spirit, we can decree a thing and know it is done no matter how trivial or how impossible it may seem to be. Jesus while on his earthly mission, lacked for nothing through His confidence that His Father provided all things for him. He could lavishly pour everything He had into those around him, on those who would accept him. When we know that the Father has already lavishly met all our needs, then we can give to others whatever their needs are without fear, worry, or anxiety. The concentration is no longer on what our needs are, but in meeting the needs of other people. That is the reason we should be living a supernatural lifestyle. That is why it is available to us now, as sons and daughters. When we know who we are, then we are no longer selfish because we know that we're provided for. Then, we can freely give of ourselves.

There was a man that came to my house. He had just been released from prison and had a fear to the point of paranoia that his every move was being watched. After a few minutes of talking to him, telling my testimony, and sharing how much the Father loved him, the fear left him. He was a changed man that quickly. It was evident he was high on drugs. Suddenly, he sobered up and had the joy of the Lord. He goes to leave the house to discover that he had locked the keys in his van. He stated that he had no money to have someone to come out. So, I just touched the van and it unlocked itself. I simply stated, "That is how much Jesus loves you." Then, he took off. I've kept in touch with him and he is now walking in the supernatural and his life has changed. Thank you, heavenly Father!

Yesterday, while at a restaurant the waitress cut herself badly enough that she was told to go to the doctor and have stitches put in it. She was telling me that she couldn't afford to lose a day's worth of wages. Grabbing her finger, I asked her, "How does it feel now?" She stated the pain had left. I let go of her finger and it had completely stopped bleeding. We are sons of God! She went back to work with a beautiful smile on her face. Thank you, Jesus!

Just so you don't get the wrong idea, you're a son/daughter of the Almighty Father. So, all of these things are yours as well. Your life can be just as full of the supernatural as mine is. I am able to focus on someone else's needs because I know mine are taken care of. This leaves me totally free to share the love of Christ as a brother of Jesus and son of the Heavenly Father.

At church one Sunday, knowing my wallet was empty, but wanting to bless the church I reached down opened my wallet and there was money, a twenty-dollar bill. Since we are provided for, we can always provide for some else's need, no matter the circumstance.

God helps those who help themselves is not in the bible or anywhere in scriptures. Those who rely on the Heavenly Father to meet their needs, their needs are met. He wants us to fully rely on him. Children should not have to meet the needs of the parents. Rather, the parents are responsible for meeting the needs of their children. With Our Heavenly Father, the same is true. We have to only believe that our needs are met so we can then share that with others. As sons and daughters, we always have the choice to have our needs met by the physical nature of things or supernaturally.

> **19** The entire universe is standing on tiptoe, yearning to see the unveiling of God's glorious sons and daughters! (Romans 8:19, TPT)

Here is the key to this verse God has already revealed who his sons and daughters are. The whole universe is waiting for us to tear the veil off and show ourselves.

> **16** For the Holy Spirit makes God's fatherhood real to us as he whispers into our innermost being, "You are God's beloved child!" **17** And since we are his true children, we qualify to share all his treasures, for indeed, we are heirs of God himself. And since we are joined to Christ, we also inherit all that he is and all that he has. We will experience being co-glorified with him provided that we accept his sufferings as our own. (Romans 8: 16-17, TPT)

The common interpretation is that we are waiting for God to reveal us to the world. But as verses sixteen and seventeen show, He already has. Now is the time for us to proudly proclaim our inheritance and start acting out who we are. We are qualified to share in all his treasures and share these treasures with others in love right now. Not in boasting in ourselves because we didn't earn the adoption, we were given the adoption. Therefore, we are to share it all freely and with the love that the Heavenly Father bestowed upon us.

We start living supernaturally when we have the revelation of who our Father is and the unadulterated version of what that means. Our Father doesn't have physical limitations. Our brother Jesus who is the house of Israel doesn't have physical limitations. Therefore, we don't either. The exception comes when we impose the limitations on ourselves by living by human wisdom and not by the wisdom of our Father. We are waiting for something to happen that has already happened.

> **18** So why fool yourself and live under an illusion? Make no mistake about it, if anyone thinks he is wise by the world's standards, he will be made wiser by being a fool for God! **19** For what the world says is wisdom is actually foolishness in God's eyes. As it is written: The cleverness of the know-it-alls becomes the trap that ensnares them. **20** And again: The Lord sees right through the clever reasonings of the wise and knows that it's all a sham. **21** So don't be proud of your allegiance to any human leader. For actually, you already have everything! It has all been given for your benefit, **22** whether it is Paul or Apollos or Peter the Rock, or whether it's the world or life or death, or whether it's the present or the future—everything belongs to you! **23** And now you are joined to the Messiah, who is joined to God. (1 Corinthians 3: 18-23, TPT)

First it must be pointed out that we shouldn't "…be proud of your allegiance to any human leader," which supports my statement earlier about the relying on a President to change things. Let's jump back to verse eighteen about living under an illusion.

What is the illusion? The illusion is that we are less than what we are. It is the illusion that we are poor, powerless, and needy. It is the belief that our Heavenly Father is unable to keep us healthy without our reliance upon physical substances. It is our belief that we must conform to the standard that our bodies will break down and wear out, that we are subject to the forces of this physical world. That is the illusion.

Will we go through trying times? Of course, we will. We aren't trying to deny that. But be encouraged Christ has overcome the world and its evil influences since He is in us. We have overcome the world, and for every problem in this world, we now have a spiritual, supernatural solution.

> **33** And everything I've taught you is so that the peace which is in me will be in you and will give you great confidence as you rest in me. For in this unbelieving world you will experience trouble and sorrows, but you must be courageous, for I have conquered the world!" (John 16:33, TPT)

We must remember that all of this was before the religious establishment of the Jewish government that denied Christ was overthrown. Yes, every one of the apostles were martyred with the exception of John. But in 70 A.D., the religious government was destroyed, and Christ was revealed as King. Remember that Jesus himself denounced that generation and government. The Jewish establishment controlled everything and denied Christ even having him crucified. They joined with the Roman Government to slay followers of Christ. It was Rome itself who then destroyed that government, and they, in turn, were destroyed.

> **5** For God will not place the coming world, of which we speak, under the government of angels. **6** But the Scriptures affirm: What is man that you would even think about him, or care about Adam's race. **7** You made him lower than the angels for a little while. You placed your glory and honor upon his head as a crown. And you have given him dominion over the works of your hands,**8** For you have placed everything under his authority. This means that God has left nothing outside the control of his Son, even if presently we have yet to see this accomplished. **9** But we see Jesus, who as a man, lived for a short time lower than the angels and has now been crowned with glorious honor because of what he suffered in his death. For it was by

> God's grace that he experienced death's bitterness on behalf of everyone! **10** For now he towers above all creation, for all things exist through him and for him. And that God made him, pioneer of our salvation, perfect through his sufferings, for this is how he brings many sons and daughters to share in his glory. **11** Jesus, the Holy One, makes us holy. And as sons and daughters, we now belong to his same Father, so he is not ashamed or embarrassed to introduce us as his brothers and sisters! **12** For he has said, "I will reveal who you really are to my brothers and sisters, and I will glorify you with praises in the midst of the congregation." **13** And, "My confidence rests in God!" And again he says, "Here I am, one with the children Yahweh has given me." **14** Since all his "children" have flesh and blood, so Jesus became human to fully identify with us. He did this, so that he could experience death and annihilate the effects of the intimidating accuser who holds against us the power of death. **15** By embracing death Jesus sets free those who live their entire lives in bondage to the tormenting dread of death. **16** For it is clear that he didn't do this for the angels, but for all the sons and daughters of Abraham. **17** This is why he had to be a Man and take hold of our humanity in every way. He made us his brothers and sisters and became our merciful and faithful King-Priest before God; as the One who removed our sins to make us one with him. **18** He suffered and endured every test and temptation, so that he can help us every time we pass through the ordeals of life. (Hebrews 2:5-18, TPT)

My friends, I would love to continue discussing this, but I have to supernaturally run to the bank. While I'm there, contemplate the above verses, not as watered-down verses, but as supernatural verse meant to show who we truly are now. We'll discuss this further in a few moments. Let's start at the top.

Jesus was made lower than angels for a short time, which means that as the Son of God and Son of Man, he walked this Earth in the same manner that we do. He wasn't walking this earth as deity, but as a man. That's in verse nine. He walked as a man and is our example of what we're capable of in Him.

Even further proof is in verse seventeen, *"This is why he had to be a man and take hold of our humanity in every way."* This is so important to understand. For those who religiously state that God doesn't share his glory with anyone, he absolutely did and does. In verse ten, *so he could share his glory with us, his sons and daughters.* We dilute and water down who we are with false humility saying we are less than who God Our Father made us to be through Jesus. To state anything different is to deny Christ and what was freely given to us. Anything else is to be antichrist because than we are denying what Jesus did. He was given control of everything and towers above everything and in him, we do too. Now all of creation is groaning waiting for us to get the revelation of who we truly are. Then, the whole world will be transformed through us.

In verse eighteen *"he suffered and endured every test and temptation, so that he can help us every time we pass through the ordeals of life."* How did Jesus endure every test and temptation even before the cross? Supernaturally is how he dealt with it, with the same authority given to us. This is the fullness that we should be walking in. Please don't give me that same old tired motto of we're only human. "But, Tony. We're adopted sons and daughters and we're grafted in. So, we are only human." Well guess what. When a plant is grafted into another plant, after a short period of time, it becomes exactly the same as the plant it was grafted into. You can't tell the difference.

We are grafted into the tree of life that is Jesus, so there is no difference. He was the first one born of many. The supernatural things should absolutely flow from us in all things.

When Paul was bitten by the serpent, did he need the agreement of another person? One of the biggest problems with Christianity is that we think we need someone else to agree with us for our healing or for something to happen. In which case, I would've been in the river without a paddle or even a boat.

The majority of times when I've been healed, it's just been myself. Most Christians, when something happens, are trying to find someone to agree with them. We don't need that. Christ in us is sufficient. You are a son/daughter of the Loving Father. You don't need anyone else to lay hands on you to be healed. That is a sign for the unbeliever or the less mature In Christ. It should be the exception not the rule.

There are times that we may need support of another person's agreement, but that should be the exception, not the rule. The same is true with the gifts of the Holy Spirit. They are for the benefit others. You have the fullness of God as a son or a daughter. So, you have everything you need in him when it comes to yourself.

Can you hear from God for yourself? Yes! What child cannot walk up to their parents and talk to them? Do you need someone else in order to communicate with a parent? No, you don't. Once again, there are times we may need another person to speak into our lives. There is no shame in that. My point is we should be striving to be complete within the Holy Spirit by ourselves. I understand that we are all at different levels of maturity. However, the goal should be to be completely reliant on the Holy Spirit inside of us without the need for another person. That is the point where we'll be able to focus our attention in ministering to other people's needs. In short, the gifts are for other people's needs. The Holy Spirit inside of us is for our needs.

> **19** After saying these things, Jesus was lifted up into heaven and sat down at the place of honor at the right hand of God!

20 And the apostles went out announcing the good news everywhere, as the Lord himself consistently worked with them, validating the message they preached with miracle-signs that accompanied them! (Mark 16:19-20, TPT)

You see the message is to the unbelievers. The miracle-signs were for the unbelievers. We as sons and daughters should already believe and walk in the supernatural, we shouldn't need convincing that Our Father is supernaturally meeting all our needs when we're in agreement with that. Yet, an unbeliever doesn't know this. If we have a need for funds, healing, a tire supernaturally repaired, a heater supernaturally fixed, we believe it, then we have it. An unbeliever doesn't know this, so they need a sign. The prodigal son's brother is an example of how most Christians are. When the prodigal son came home, he needed a sign that he was loved and restored. The father doing everything he did including throwing the feast confirmed to the son that he was restored. Meanwhile, the older son who never left was upset because the father never threw him a feast. It was because the older son had access to all these things already. We already have access to the supernatural, so the supernatural isn't a sign to us, it should be a way of life.

Worksheet: Chapter 7

1. Jesus is the first born of many. Who is the many?

2. During Jesus earthly ministry, He operated as what?

3. What is the illusion that most people have?

4. Does God share his glory? If so, how did he share his glory?

5. Watering down who we are In Christ does what in our lives?

6. Describe what inheritance we have as sons and daughters?

7. Make a list of traits that we should have in common with Jesus as a brother.

NOTES:

8. Mysteries Unveiled

Making the connection that we are sons and daughters of the Father of the universe, goes a long way in walking in the supernatural. Indeed, the Christianese language would be "walking in the spirit." But to the majority of believers, walking in the spirit, means only a code of morality, not the supernatural. By its very implication "walking in the spirit" is supernatural. God is Spirit. This means everything he does is supernatural by our limited minds. Therefore, if we are walking in the spirit, we are then to be walking supernaturally.

Then the pharisaic or religious mindset sets in: "Well, His ways are higher than our ways. You don't know if God intended us to walk that way. God is mysterious. Who can know the things of God? If God wants something done, He'll just do it (We've already discussed how He always works through us)." That is the churchy and pharisaic way of thinking.

In this chapter, we'll prove that there are no more mysteries left to be solved. All has been revealed to us through his spirit, whose temple we are. In fact, Jesus told his disciples just that prior to the cross. They were still dazed, confused, and didn't get that at the time just as the majority doesn't get it today when they operate under the mind of Adam and the physical senses. The physical mind, the brain, tells us we have physical limitations. So, we believe what we see instead of believing who we are. Just the fact that in order to prove this to you, there will have to be overwhelming proof, shows how many of us operate from the mind of Adam. Because right now, you may be thinking that God is still keeping things a mystery. He isn't. Coffee time while you chew on this scripture, one of many in this chapter:

> **11** He said to them, "The privilege of intimately knowing the mystery of God's kingdom realm has been granted to you, but not to the others, where everything is revealed in parables. (Mark 4:11, TPT)

Did you see that intimately knowing the mystery of God's kingdom was granted to the disciples? Jesus said this even while the disciples weren't understanding it. Notice also, that even to those not granted this privilege, it was still revealed in the form of parables. This wasn't Jesus or the Father hiding anything from them, it was because he wanted them to be able to understand it. The majority of people, including the religious leaders couldn't understand. They had the mindset of the world:

> **15** I have never called you 'servants,' because a master doesn't confide in his servants, and servants don't always understand what the master is doing. But I call you my most intimate friends, for I reveal to you everything that I've heard from my Father. (John 15:15, TPT)

Jesus said this even before the cross, before his spirit was poured out on all flesh. At this time, we weren't given the status of sons and daughters. Now, we have that status when we accept it. For example, a child may be born to a royal family. If that child is swept away from the family and never knows that he is royalty, he still is a prince but doesn't know that. That child then never knows the full inheritance he has. This is where we've been because we've been under the false impression that there are mysteries not revealed to us. The following fourteen verses show that these mysteries have been revealed:

> **25** I give all my praises and glory to the one who has more than enough power to make you strong and keep you steadfast through the promises found in the wonderful news that I preach; that is, the proclamation of Jesus, the Anointed One. This wonderful news includes the unveiling of the mystery kept secret from the dawn of creation until now. (Romans 16:25, TPT)
>
> **51** Listen, and I will tell you a divine mystery: not all of us will die, but we will all be transformed. (1 Corinthians 15:51, TPT)
>
> **9** God has now revealed to us his mysterious will regarding Christ—which is to fulfill his own good plan. (Ephesians 1:9, NLT)
>
> **3** As I briefly wrote earlier, God himself revealed his mysterious plan to me. **4** As you read what I have written, you will understand my insight into this plan regarding Christ. (Ephesians 3:3-4, NLT)
>
> **9** I was chosen to explain to everyone this mysterious plan that God, the Creator of all things, had kept secret from the beginning. (Ephesians 3:9, NLT)

32 This is a great mystery, but it is an illustration of the way Christ and the church are one. (Ephesians 5:32, NLT)

✓ **19** And pray for me, too. Ask God to give me the right words so I can boldly explain God's mysterious plan that the Good News is for Jews and Gentiles alike. (Ephesians 6:19, NLT)

26 This message was kept secret for centuries and generations past, but now it has been revealed to God's people. **27** For God wanted them to know that the riches and glory of Christ are for you Gentiles, too. And this is the secret: Christ lives in you. This gives you assurance of sharing his glory. (Colossians 1:26-27, NLT)

2 I want them to be encouraged and knit together by strong ties of love. I want them to have complete confidence that they understand God's mysterious plan, which is Christ himself. (Colossians 2:2, NLT)

3 Pray for us, too, that God will give us many opportunities to speak about his mysterious plan concerning Christ. That is why I am here in chains. (Colossians 4:3, NLT)

9 They must be committed to the mystery of the faith now revealed and must live with a clear conscience. (1 Timothy 3:9, NLT)

16 Without question, this is the great mystery of our faith: Christ was revealed in a human body and vindicated by the Spirit. He was seen by angels and announced to the nations. He was believed in throughout the world and taken to heaven in glory. (1 Timothy 3:16, NLT)

> **1** So, look at Apollos and me as mere servants of Christ who have been put in charge of explaining God's mysteries. (1 Corinthians 4:1, NLT)

Do you see that all of God's mysteries were already revealed? What about the scripture, "My ways are higher than your ways, my thoughts are higher than your thoughts?" There are two scriptures in Isaiah that are used to say that we can't possibly know the things of God. Well guess what? The answer to this shows how living before Christ was much different under the Law of Moses than what we have in the New Covenant. This was true to say before Christ. After Christ, it is a way to stay locked into religion, not knowing our relationship as sons and daughters.

> **13** Who is able to advise the Spirit of the Lord? Who knows enough to give him advice or teach him? (Isaiah 40:13, NLT)

> **4** For since the beginning of the world men have not heard, nor perceived by the ear, neither hath the eye seen, O God, beside thee, what he hath prepared for him that waiteth for him. (Isaiah 64:4, KJV)

> **8** For my thoughts are not your thoughts, neither are your ways my ways, saith the Lord. **9** For as the heavens are higher than the earth, so are my ways higher than your ways, and my thoughts than your thoughts. (Isaiah 55:8-9, NLT)

Watch this! Two verses are going to show the huge difference between before and after the cross and our access to all knowledge and wisdom of the loving, Heavenly Father through Christ. There are no longer any mysteries, His thoughts can indeed be our thoughts and we truly are one with him.

> **16** For Who has ever intimately known the mind of the Lord Yahweh well enough to become his counselor? Christ has, and we possess Christ's perceptions. (1 Corinthians 2:16, TPT)

> **8** None of the rulers of this present world order understood it, for if they had, they never would have crucified the Lord of shining glory. **9** This is why the Scriptures say: Things never discovered or heard of before, things beyond our ability to imagine these are the many things God has in store for all his lovers. **10** But God now unveils these profound realities to us by the Spirit. Yes, he has revealed to us his inmost heart and deepest mysteries through the Holy Spirit, who constantly explores all things. (1 Corinthians 2:8-10, TPT)

We go around saying "Oh God works in mysterious ways." Yet, scripture after the Cross shows us something completely different. Who can know the thoughts of God? Christ! And we now possess Christ's perceptions, so we have it. Bottom line is, realize this: the veil is now ripped from our faces. Now, it is the Holy Spirit who reveals to us all things. That we are now one with God just as Christ is. The deepest mysteries and his heart, all of it, is made known to us when we seek it out for ourselves. As sons and daughters, therefore, we have the gift which is the Holy Spirit. Again, we no longer need to seek out another person for his knowledge and wisdom.

What I really want to convey to you is that, as you get the heart revelation of these things, you no longer have to seek another person for healing or any other miraculous thing. All you need is the One who is inside of you. The gifts of the Holy Spirit are meant for believers who are young and still on milk as well as for unbelievers. As we graduate from the mind of Adam into the mind of Christ, we should be providing the miraculous to others, having no need to seek it for ourselves because we are living in the supernatural, naturally.

> **5** And if anyone longs to be wise, ask God for wisdom and he will give it! He won't see your lack of wisdom as an opportunity to scold you over your failures but he will overwhelm your failures with his generous grace. (James 1:5, TPT)

Wisdom is the lack of mystery. If we are wise in a topic, then there is no mystery left in it. Ask God for wisdom and he will give it. This is further proof that in the New Covenant, there are no more mysteries unless you think there are.

While writing this, my area was put on a tornado warning and my wife was listening to the local weather. She called to me and told me. Almost in mid-sentence, the weatherman had to change what he was saying, which was there was circular motions that was a tornado forming. He then stated that it appeared that a tornado was now not likely, but that there were strong winds of 60 miles an hour. I actually went on Marco Polo with a friend and showed him how calm it was. That is an awesome example of being a son of God. I didn't have the need to call a prayer hotline and ask thousands of people to pray for this area, nor did I have to pray to God for the gift of working miracles. We already have him inside of us. I didn't even have to seek someone out who had the gift of working of miracles. Yet, did others in this area receive a miracle gift? Yes, and most are unaware of it, presumably. Since we are talking about the gifts of the Holy Spirit, let's get it on. This is very important to understand in walking in the supernatural. If you feel the gifts are exclusive to certain people, then you will fall short of experiencing this and not reach the fullness of Christ as well as if you believe each person is only given one or two specific gifts. That way of thinking is balderdash.

> **4** It is the same Holy Spirit who continues to distribute many different varieties of gifts. **5** The Lord Yahweh is one, and he is the one who apportions to believers' different varieties of ministries. **6** The same God distributes different kinds of miracles that accomplish different results through each believer's gift and ministry as he energizes and activates them. **7** Each believer is given continuous revelation by the Holy Spirit to benefit not just himself but all. **8** For example: The Spirit gives to one the gift of the word of wisdom. To another, the same Spirit gives the gift of the word of revelation knowledge. **9** And to another, the same Spirit gives the gift of faith. And to another, the same Spirit gives gifts of healing. **10** And to another the power to work miracles. And to another the gift of prophecy. And to another the gift to discern what the Spirit is speaking. And to another the gift of speaking different kinds of tongues. And to another the gift of interpretation of tongues. **11** Remember, it is the same Holy Spirit who distributes, activates, and operates these different gifts as he chooses for each believer. (1 Corinthians 12:4-11, TPT)

Verses eight through eleven these are talking about special abilities. These are as the need arises, not meant as an exclusive gift to one specific believer. If I'm standing in front of a person (say at Walmart) that needs a word of knowledge, he gives me that word of knowledge to give as a gift to that person. Then as I'm walking out to the parking lot, there's a person that needs to receive a gift of healing. Therefore, the Holy Spirit uses me to give healing to that person. There are two specific sentences within these verses that clarifies this. *Each believer is given continuous revelation to benefit not himself, but for the benefit of all.* In other words, the Holy Spirit is giving me the revelation that this person needs a miracle, that person needs the gift of healing, the next person needs a gift of wisdom. Then in verse eleven, *Remember, it is the same Holy Spirit who distributes, activates, and operates these different gifts as he chooses for each believer.* As he chooses for each believer. In other words, we all have access to each gift according to the need of the person that we are in contact with. The New Living Translation puts it, "*A spiritual gift is given to each of us so we can help each other.*"

The common way that it is mistaught does not make any sense. If I'm at a Walmart and the person I'm talking to needs a prophetic word, then my response is supposed to be, "Sorry, I can't help you because I don't have the gift of prophecy." Of course, what most people think is the gift of prophecy is actually a word of wisdom.

Prophecy in the New Testament as defined by Paul is a word meant to build up, motivate, or comfort. A word of wisdom is to direct one's path by a word of what's in store in the future for that person. In just a few chapters over, Paul tells us to desire all the gifts of the Spirit, especially to prophesy. "*Let love be your highest goal! But you should also desire the special abilities the Spirit gives—especially the ability to prophesy. (1 Corinthians 14:1, NLT).*" With this being the truth, either Paul contradicts himself or the common interpretation of this set of scriptures is wrong. You can't have it both ways. In fact, in verse thirty-one he states the same thing.

Can you imagine Jesus saying, "Nope, I can't give you an encouraging word. Go look up Jim Bob for an encouraging word. We haven't even mentioned the fact that Jesus told us that these signs will follow those who believe. So, does every single believer have the special ability to heal the sick, or is Paul contradicting Jesus? I think not! It is those that are wrongly teaching this set of scriptures that are contradicting Jesus. Let's move along to the gifts of services.

> **12** Just as the human body is one, though it has many parts that together form one body, so too is Christ. **13** For by one Spirit we all were immersed and mingled into one single

> body. And no matter our status—whether we are Jews or non-Jews, oppressed or free—we are all privileged to drink deeply of the same Holy Spirit. (1 Corinthians 12:12-13, TPT)

In the above scripture Paul is switching gears to the service gifts. Pay extreme attention to the comparison. "And no matter our status, whether we are Jews or non-Jews, oppressed or free, we are all privileged to drink deeply of the same Holy Spirit." In other words, we can all operate in the same gifts of service.

> **22** In fact, the weaker our parts, the more vital and essential they are. **23** The body parts we think are less honorable we treat with greater respect. And the body parts that need to be covered in public we treat with propriety and clothe them. **24** But some of our body parts don't require as much attention. Instead, God has mingled the body parts together, giving greater honor to the "lesser" members who lacked it. **25** He has done this intentionally so that every member would look after the others with mutual concern, and so that there will be no division in the body. **26** In that way, whatever happens to one member happens to all. If one suffers, everyone suffers. If one is honored, everyone rejoices. **27** You are the body of the Anointed One, and each of you is a unique and vital part of it. **28** God has placed in the church the following: First apostles, second prophets, third teachers, then those with gifts of miracles, gifts of divine healing, gifts of revelation knowledge, gifts of leadership, and gifts of different kinds of tongues. **29** Not everyone is an apostle or a prophet or a teacher. Not everyone performs miracles **30** or has gifts of healing or speaks in tongues or interprets tongues. **31** But you should all constantly boil over with passion in seeking the higher

> gifts. And now I will show you a superior way to live that is beyond comparison. (1 Corinthians 12:22-31, TPT)

The gifts of service are to lift up the lesser body parts, in other words, the less mature. Pay attention to twenty-two through twenty-six. That is the reason for the different services, to clothe and pay greater honor to the lesser. It's all for the benefit of the body to raise up everyone to the stature of Jesus. There isn't one person owns any one of the gifts of services. We can and should at various times operate in each one of these gifts. But because of the way we view the "modern church," we don't recognize that.

Now down to verse twenty-nine. "*Not everyone is an apostle or a prophet or a teacher.*" Of course not. This is because we're all at different levels of our walk. So, not everyone is operating as an apostle, but all can. When I first became a believer and hadn't read the bible yet, was I able to be a teacher? No, but now I am. Now check out thirty-one "*But you should all constantly boil over with passion in seeking the higher gifts.*" Paul is not going to tell anyone to seek something that God won't grant them. All of the special ability and service gifts are meant to push up those who have a lack in specific areas. Stop using your western, modern-minded thinking in order to understand the gifts of the Spirit. The church structure was whole communities in those days. Not a hundred different church buildings within a community. It was the whole city. Why do you think that Paul wrote a letter to the city of Corinth? It wasn't a hierarchy either, rather everyone contributing. We think the listing of these services is in order of importance and that's the way the majority of churches operate Yet, Paul himself would tell you that he is the least, not the greatest. "*But some of our body parts require lesser attention. Giving greater honor to the lesser members who lacked it.*" In a modern church it is those who are in the services that expect and require more attention and honor. C'mon you know I'm speaking truth here. One last bit of proof that all can and should operate in every gift. In spite of the way translations may make it sound is this scripture: **24** *This is the reason I urge you to boldly believe for whatever you ask for in prayer—believe that you have received it and it will be yours. (Mark 11:24, TPT)* End of story. Argue with the translators, not Jesus.

We are each one of us to be operating in the supernatural. I dislike the term. We are spiritual beings. Let's put it like this we are spiritual beings who are giving life to our dwelling. So, the dwelling shouldn't influence the spiritual being. It is the spiritual being that influences the dwelling.

Take for example a brick and mortar house, it is lifeless without an owner living in it. It has no power of its own and is subject to what an owner wants to do with it. If the owner decides he wants to move walls around, that is what happens. With our bodies we think that it is our bodies that control how abundantly we live our lives. Time to change that way of thinking.

It is our spirit that should be the influence as to how abundant our life is, with the Holy Spirit, who is our spirit, the greatest influence of all. Likewise, since we are spiritual beings, we are to influence the world. In Christ, we have authority over all things in this world. The spiritual influences are not separate in the physical world, they are the very foundation of the physical world. Without spirit, the world is lifeless. Nothing exists outside of the spiritual world because the Creator and Father who spoke it into being is Spirit. In fact, here's a little thought-provoking statement. In Christ we are actually higher than the angels, yet people look at angels as being higher and more powerful than we are. Many people seek them, and ask them to do things, the stories of seeing angels always entice people's imagination. Yet, we are one with Christ, which they can never be. Think on that for a moment.

Worksheet: Chapter 8

1. Name three of the many mysteries that have been revealed to us.

____
____
____
____
____

2. If any man lack wisdom, let him ask God for it. What is God's answer?

____
____
____

3. Name three things that changed dramatically in the New Covenant. The animal sacrifices are a given, so that don't count!

____
____
____
____

4. What is the reason for the gifts of the Holy Spirit? How many are available to each person?

____
____
____
____

____

____

5. Who is the greatest in the Kingdom of God?

____

____

6. This is a challenge: Choose one gift of the Holy Spirit for each day of the week. Ask the Holy Spirit to operate in that particular gift for that day. Believe that you have received it. Then approach at least one person and present them with that gift. Write down your experience below.

____

____

____

____

____

7. When there is a threatening storm system, tell it to dissolve. You can do this with a group of believers or even with a young child. Write down your experience, below.

____

____

____

____

____

9. Living from the Spirit of Christ

Living from the Spirit of Christ is key to all of this. It isn't in trusting the physical things of this world. If you place what you see with your physical senses as the ruling truth, then it will be. There is a greater truth that supersedes the physical order of life on this Earth that is dependent on what you believe in your heart. Without the renewing of your mind to these truths, the supernatural will be sporadic at best. We were created to be supernatural beings. Now we are reborn in spirit. Yet, many are still subject to the information brought in through the physical senses and stored in our brain. God did not create this duplicity, we did. That is the bad news.

Here's the good news. The Loving Father gave us the answer since we are now sons and daughters, the Holy Spirit. Once again, the problem is that we still look to the physical things for the answer instead of looking inside our spirit where the Holy One is giving us the answers. We look up to heaven for the Father to come down and give us the answers through a human voice or sight. We are looking for the answers externally on the Earth instead of internally trusting the person of the Holy Spirit. Unfortunately.

Most believers renew their minds to what is sin and are focused on "not sinning" instead of what the Holy Spirit is saying. We also focus on sickness and death instead of the life we have in God's Kingdom which is why most believers are powerless, feel defeated, and are waiting to be supernaturally raptured instead of walking as sons and daughters now and releasing blessings throughout their daily lives. Instead of being in God's Rest, they are fighting and chasing their tails around in circles. Oops! Did I say that?

> **26** But when the Father sends the Spirit of Holiness, the One like me who sets you free, he will teach you all things in my name. And he will inspire you to remember every word that I've told you. (John 14:26, TPT)

The Holy Spirit inside of us is the teacher. Yes, he does use things like human teachers and scriptures. But those exterior things are supposed to lead us into being reliant on the Holy Spirit while receiving all truths directly from Him. Instead of growing independent of physical resources for truth, we become stuck on only depending on those things. By that I mean human teachers and, yes, the Bible. The scriptures are an external source of laying the foundation of Christ and also open to interpretation.

> **16** Every Scripture has been written by the Holy Spirit, the breath of God. It will empower you by its instruction and correction, giving you the strength to take the right direction and lead you deeper into the path of godliness. **17** Then you will be God's servant, fully mature and perfectly prepared to fulfill any assignment God gives you. (2 Timothy 3:16-17, TPT)

Scripture is the means to arrive to the end goal, not the end goal itself. Relationship with God cannot be solely based on scriptures. Scripture should lead us into the relationship but isn't a relationship on its own. The relationship is the Holy Spirit and walking in the spirit is our path with Him. We tend to view scriptures as the end all authority. They are not. They are a guide that will help to keep us on track, but the end all authority is Holy Spirit inside of us. Proof of this is that there are people that know God's Word in Greek, Aramaic, Latin and can quote them all, but lead powerless lives.

Deeper into the path of godliness is relationship. People often yearn for the days when God led the children of Israel by cloud during the day and a pillar of fire at night. They think because of this they were closer to God than we are. Because he showed himself. That couldn't be farther from the truth. We have him inside of us leading the way, but few people ever come to this realization.

The bible and scriptures are not supernatural nor are they the incorruptible seed of God. The bible is the greatest book ever put together, it is one that I cherish and love. But it is a book, the book itself has no power to save. Many people idolize the book, thinking it will solve all their problems. It won't, it can't, and it doesn't. In fact, one statement that was thrown at me recently was "scriptures are the only physical thing we have of God on this earth." This statement is untrue.

> **18** But God shows his anger from heaven against all sinful, wicked people who suppress the truth by their wickedness. **19** They know the truth about God because he has made it obvious to them. 20 For ever since the world was created, people have seen the earth and sky. Through everything God made, they can clearly see his invisible qualities—his eternal power and divine nature. So they have no excuse for not knowing God. (Romans 1:18-20, NLT)

We have all of creation pointing directly to God and, furthermore:

> **39** "You are busy analyzing the Scriptures, frantically poring over them in hopes of gaining eternal life. Everything you read points to me, 40 yet you still refuse to come to me so I can give you the life you're looking for—eternal life! (John 5:39-40, TPT)

Jesus was talking to the Pharisees who knew scriptures inside and out. Yet, they refused to believe in the Messiah. And many a Sunday preacher stands up holding a Bible and state, "This is the incorruptible seed of God." No, it isn't.

The written word can be corrupted by poor translations, misinterpretation, not knowing the culture during the time it was written, and taking it out of context. In many ways, it can be corrupted because it is a physical thing called a book. The incorruptible Word of God is Jesus who is now in us as the Holy Spirit.

> **23** For through the eternal and living Word of God you have been born again. And this "seed" that he planted within you can never be destroyed but will live and grow inside of you forever. For: (1 Peter 1:23, TPT)

Would I ever do without scriptures? No! I love scriptures, thank God for them, and always encourage people to study them for themselves. But without the Holy Spirit inside of us, the words on the page do nothing and mean nothing. As the Pharisees themselves prove, they can lead straight to religion without relationship. And religion without relationship is unyielding, harsh, cruel, without mercy, and causes other people to die as this passage states:

> **12** For we have the living Word of God, which is full of energy, and it pierces more sharply than a two-edged sword. It will even penetrate to the very core of our being where soul and spirit, bone and marrow meet! It interprets and reveals the true thoughts and secret motives of our hearts. (Hebrews 4:12, TPT)

Word in the Greek is Logos which means the spoken word by a living person, the Holy Spirit, not the written word. It is the Holy Spirit who makes the written word come alive. It is the Holy Spirit who interprets and reveals the true thoughts and secrets of our heart. The Holy Spirit, who is inside of us, is directing our path when we are walking in the spirit. It isn't a personality change, although we do change as a person. Our personality stays the same. The Holy Spirit resides in us, so he conforms to our personality. If in church we act in a way we wouldn't act in public, then it's our perception of walking in spirit that is presenting itself, not the Holy Spirit. And I'm not talking about dancing, or having sudden energy, or laughing. I do all those things inside and outside of church. But there is a craziness that can happen inside the church that isn't God, when there is a sudden personality change. Let the Holy Spirit give you the revelation of what I'm implying here. I'm getting a cup of coffee while you ask him for the wisdom of the revelation that is meant.

The Heavenly Father no longer has to come down from Heaven, nor do our prayers have to go up to Heaven. The Father no longer has to hear the cries of his people from way up there and then come down to earth to inhabit the praise of his people. There isn't a coming down at all now. He is in us. In order, for the supernatural to happen in a continual flow, we must make a change in our thinking. He must become a real being inside of us, not a person who is externally somewhere else that must come down. We must be aware that he is always in us and we don't have to wait for him to know our thoughts and needs. He is alive and active inside of us, not waiting to jump out of written words. He's the one who makes the words jump out at you because he is alive and active within. All that going up and coming down is what happened prior to the day of Pentecost.

We often use the psalm 22:3, *"But thou art holy, O thou that inhabitest the praises of Israel,"* in a way that implies that if you are praising God, he comes down from heaven to hear you. The praise causes him to come down.

As a temple of the Holy Spirit the praise that is inhabited is from within, going outward through your voice into the world. Praise then changes your internal thermostat, then that changes the atmosphere around you. We can't use scriptures in the Old Testament the same way without transforming them through the filter of being sons and daughters and of being one with the Lord now. Those who served God back then were servants of God, not sons and daughters, and not the temple. In order to experience the supernatural consistently, there must be that transformation of mindset. Everything in the Old Testament was about what was coming. In the New Testament, it's about what has happened and who we are. There are so many scriptures from prior to Jesus' resurrection that we take and use in the same way they are written. This is so not correct.

The Gospels are still under the Law of Moses. Jesus was born under the Law and fulfilled the Law. He often spoke as under the Law of Moses. For instance:

> **17** "If you think I've come to set aside the law of Moses or the writings of the prophets, you're mistaken. I have come to fulfill and bring to perfection all that has been written. **18** Indeed, I assure you, as long as heaven and earth endure,

> not even the smallest detail of the Law will be done away with until its purpose is complete. (Matthew 5:17-18, TPT)

Guess what? We can't look at that as if we're still waiting for it to happen. It's already happened. Jesus also stated that his body would be destroyed and after three days he shall rise again. His resurrection has already happened. So, if we don't transform our mind-set, then it's as if we're still waiting on His resurrection. If we're stuck on Jesus telling his disciples not to go into any city other than those in Israel, then we miss where He tells the disciples to go into all the nations after His resurrection. This is where we fail miserably. We don't look at scriptures and see where the transformation occurred. So, we're still stuck looking at things with the mind of Adam as if we're still lacking and waiting. Another one that is often heard from the pulpit is we want God's glory to come down from heaven. Got some news for you. God's glory doesn't fall down from heaven anymore. It comes from inside the believers who are present and out into the Earth. We are God's glory therefore it's from inside our spirit to the outside world. The supernatural is the same way. It works from inside the believer to the outside world, changing earthly circumstances. If you are looking for the supernatural to occur but you're looking for it to fall from heaven, then it is very likely you will keep waiting.

Walking in the spirit starts by recognizing the love of the Father towards us. We look at love as an action that starts by us initiating love and expect it to be given back. With the Father, it starts with His divine love toward us. When we recognize His love toward us, we accept his son and are joined with him. He places his incorruptible seed (Holy Spirit) within us, and then it is Holy Spirit who brings us into perfection through his love in us. That is how faith is activated.

> **6** When you're placed into the Anointed One and joined to him, circumcision and religious obligations can benefit you

> nothing. All that matters now is living in the faith that is activated and brought to perfection by love. (Galations 5:6, TPT)

When we know this love we want more, and we start communication with the Holy Spirit inside of us. This is internal, not external. By that I mean that we don't have to reach into the outside world to draw him into us. We don't need a sermon or music to initiate this communication. And it is much deeper than simply asking or begging. Often times, there is no earthly language involved. There doesn't need to be. When we are one with something, you automatically know it intimately. There is no need for words.

We'd better back up to before we became believers. First, I truly do believe that innately we are aware of God, without an outside introduction, the moment we're born. As Romans One indicates, outside influences then come in. In my case, it was being shown a God who hated us and was judging every move we made. Then, hearing how God causes tragedies to test us. It was that god that I rejected when I became an atheist. Yet, deep down I knew that there was a creator. Still, I couldn't reconcile what I innately knew with what I was being shown about the Creator, nor could I understand how a person could serve a god that would send a son to be punished for all of people's sin. Poor Jesus! To have such a cruel Father, and he was happy to do it. Wow! Then, I met a woman who, not by words, but by her actions, demonstrated the Love of the Father. Yet, I still couldn't reconcile a number of things. Until my healing, I had accepted Christ the best I could at that time. This was without a relationship, simply punching a ticket.

Even without relationship, I experienced a huge miracle, my healing from ALS. That is how available miracles are. We have the miracle inside of us. This is the love of the Father towards us. When we have a revelation of that love, then we start walking in the spirit.

Simply put, it is knowing our internal needs are met by the Holy Spirit in us. When we know our internal needs are met then the fruit of the spirit flows out of us. We stop looking to the outside external circumstances to meet our needs and just know they've already been met. When we do this then our outside actions reflect the internal divine love. Our actions and lifestyle then show this.

> **22–23** But the fruit produced by the Holy Spirit within you is divine love in all its varied expressions:
>
> joy that overflows,
>
> peace that subdues,
>
> patience that endures,
>
> kindness in action,
>
> a life full of virtue,
>
> faith that prevails,
>
> gentleness of heart, and
>
> strength of spirit.
>
> Never set the law above these qualities, for they are meant to be limitless. (Galations 5:22-23, TPT)

What blocks this fruit is when we set the law above these qualities. In other words, we base it off our actions. We try to prove to God and others how much we love God. We try to create joy in ourselves. However, this joy we create is based on our own actions (When we feel God is happy with us because we're doing such good). All of these things, when we try (unknowingly) to create them, are false forms of them mostly based off of emotions and outside circumstances.

When we aren't trying to create these expressions of love, they literally flow out of us unimpeded. That is when we are walking in the spirit. That is also when the miraculous simply starts to happen. Faith that prevails, strength of spirit, are the catalyst to the supernatural. Once again, those two are part of the expressions of His Divine Love towards us, not as a result of our love towards him. When we are purposely trying to operate in the supernatural, to have a need met that is when nothing apparently happens. When we know our internal needs are met, then we know the external needs are met (before it actually happens). That's when the fruit of the spirit is flowing out of us and the supernatural spontaneously happens. It starts from our spirit to the outside world and is all based on His Divine Love that is installed in us, by the Holy Spirit.

The best way I can truly explain this is from my own experience. My own healing came about through the vision I had. I experienced His Love for me at that moment. Then, after my healing, based on knowing all my internal needs were met my life started flowing in holiness and unreal supernatural power even before I read scriptures.

Then, I started studying scriptures and immersed myself in them. For three years, I was on cloud nine! Nothing phased me. Then I started studying the Old Testament and the ten commandments. I spent time around people that stressed the ten commandments, taught that you better not sin, etc. Religiousness in other words. Without realizing it, I started basing things off of my actions. This blocked the fruit of the spirit and my internal thermostat was turned off. For a short time, the supernatural and my moral actions no longer just flowed out of me with ease. That is what happens when we base things off of our actions (our righteousness). It is also why, when we place more importance on the written word of

God than on the Holy Spirit, things suddenly become more difficult. Which is why in the first paragraphs of this chapter, I made the comments about scripture. Scripture is a huge part of my daily life and the wisdom within it is crucial. But if we aren't letting the Holy Spirit within us guide and impart his wisdom into us, then it can impede us. If we're only living from the written word, then it becomes strict adherence to the law, and both living in holiness and walking in the supernatural becomes strenuous. Let's face it, most Christians are living their lives from their perception of the written word (or the perception of their pastor), which is why most Christians are powerless. We are trying to perform based off the written word instead of letting the Holy Spirit produce the fruit of divine love in us. We try to set the thermostat of whether our internal needs are met instead of letting Him set it. That's when we flow from it.

I tell you the truth, it would have been easier if I had never read the Old Testament. It is likely that I would still be in the state I was in the first three years of my walk with Christ. But then again, I wouldn't have the more complete understanding that I have now to share with others. There are too many preachers who focus on the outside actions instead of teaching that divine love is already installed in us. We will be in obedience when we allow the fruit to flow in the knowledge that our inner needs are met, and we are complete in him.

> **9** "I love each of you with the same love that the Father loves me. You must continually let my love nourish your hearts. **10** If you keep my commands, you will live in my love, just as I have kept my Father's commands, for I continually live nourished and empowered by his love. **11** My purpose for telling you these things is so that the joy that I experience will fill your hearts with overflowing gladness! (John 15: 9-11, TPT)

The most important part to look at in this verse is, "you must continually let my love nourish your hearts." That's the internal need, love. The eternal expressions are all contained within His love, then we will keep His commands. Jesus states, "…for I continually live nourished and empowered by his love." I know how that comes across when read in context. But look at it this way. The word for is a conjunction meaning because or since. Substituting one of the other words clarifies what Jesus meant. "Just as I have kept my Father's commands, since/because I continually live nourished and empowered by his love." It's His love that empowers us, not our love for him. Now, our internal thermostat is set, and we walk in the spirit which means a holy and a supernatural life.

Worksheet: Chapter 9

1. Who is the incorruptible Word of God?

____
____
____
____
____
____

2. Who is the incorruptible seed?

____
____
____
____
____
____

3. It is possible to live a holy and supernatural lifestyle without the written word (see my own testimony), but without who is it impossible to live out that lifestyle?

____
____
____
____
____
____

4. What does the Holy Spirit give us that sets our internal thermostat?

5. What blocks the flow of the fruit of the Spirit?

6. In your own words describe what is "walking in the Spirit?"

7. The supernatural is the result of what?

8. Have you completed the challenges from Chapter 8? If yes, repeat them with the knowledge you gained from this chapter. Record the difference in your experiences, this time.

____
____
____
____
____
____

9. What were the benefits for you, from this chapter?

____
____
____
____
____
____

10. Citizen of the Kingdom of God

Let's talk about the Kingdom of God and the Kingdom of Heaven. These are not separate. They are one in the same. Earth is no longer separate from heaven. It is a part of heaven. There is the unseen dimension and the seen, but there is no separation between them. The unseen created what is seen. Therefore, both exist in this physical world. The 'things unseen' dimension is what holds the physical world together. There wouldn't be a physical world without the spiritual dimension. Yet, we are so careful to separate them when there is no separation. We can't see electricity. Yet, we see the effect of it when we turn a light on. It is the same with the spiritual dimension. We may not be able to see it, but we can definitely see the effects of it. Our bodies come alive because our spirit is in them. Without our spirit they are empty shells that turn to dust. When we quit separating the spiritual from the physical, then operating in the supernatural becomes easier.

It's about being one with the Father, Son, Holy Spirit, and each other. Unity is such a huge word in scriptures. If a person sees themselves on the outside looking in or trying to reach out from a distance, then it takes a striving to reach it. The supernatural isn't reached by striving, but by resting in unity with the Holy Spirit. Which is why separating and compartmentalizing the spiritual world from the physical world is error. We have what we need long before the need arises, but because we think there is a separation of spirit from the physical world, we fall into striving to get. Then, we fall into choosing the physical path to take care of our own needs. When we separate the two, what we feel we have In Christ is diluted down and then put off to the future "when we get to heaven."

> **3** Every spiritual blessing in the heavenly realm has already been lavished upon us as a love gift from our wonderful heavenly Father, the Father of our Lord Jesus—all because he sees us wrapped into Christ. This is why we celebrate him with all our hearts! (Ephesians 1: 3, TPT)

We read verses like this one as if someday when we get to heaven, we'll receive every spiritual blessing. We totally skip over that it has already been lavished upon us. Notice also where unity with Christ comes in. We are wrapped into Christ. Therefore, as he is, so are we now! Every spiritual blessing now includes the physical needs because of our oneness with Christ.

> **4** And he chose us to be his very own, joining us to himself even before he laid the foundation of the universe! Because of his great love, he ordained us, so that we would be seen as holy in his eyes with an unstained innocence. (Ephesians 1:4, TPT)

Do you see where unity and seeing ourselves as unified with the Father is so huge? He joined us to himself with such unity there is an unbreakable bond that makes all spiritual blessings available to us now, in this physical existence. What need did Jesus not have provided for him while in his earthly ministry? What was unavailable to him? Since all his needs were already met, his only focus became serving the needs of others all accomplished supernaturally in every aspect of the word supernaturally. We often skip over another important point:

> **25** Jesus did countless things that I haven't included here. And if every one of his works were written down and described one by one, I suppose that the world itself wouldn't have enough room to contain the books that would have to be written! (John 21:25, TPT)

Take a moment and ponder on this. The world itself couldn't contain the books that would have to be written. This was in just three and a half years! With that being stated, with us being in Unity, with the Father and Son, what in the world is unattainable for us? Therefore, the next time you experience a physical symptom and you go to call a doctor, have the thought first, "I'm unified with Jesus therefore my health needs are already met." Then, go to the doctor and since your health needs are met, you speak health over those in the doctor's office. They get healed and you get a clean bill of health. When your first thought is being unified with Christ, then you have nothing to be anxious for. This is true for every area of your life. In fact, we can go so far to say that even when Jesus needed transportation, it was provided for him. Since donkey was provided for him, even that is available for us. Here is another key. As I've continually stressed throughout this book. We are provided for so that we can meet others' needs. This isn't about a selfish message, rather a selfless message. Let's continue to explore how unified with Christ we are:

> **7** Since we are now joined to Christ, we have been given the treasures of redemption by his blood—the total cancellation

> of our sins—all because of the cascading riches of his grace. **8** This superabundant grace is already powerfully working in us, releasing within us all forms of wisdom and practical understanding. (Ephesians 1: 7-8, TPT)

We are joined to Christ means we have freedom from all bondage powerfully working within us. Releasing all forms of wisdom means all forms of wisdom, Christians. Instead, we rationalize that word to mean anything but all. We have access to God's Wisdom now, which all Our Heavenly Father knows is the supernatural, because that is who He is. We are so conformed to the world that we're under human wisdom, not God's Wisdom.

> **18** I pray that the light of God will illuminate the eyes of your imagination, flooding you with light, until you experience the full revelation of the hope of his calling — that is, the wealth of God's glorious inheritances that he finds in us, his holy ones! **19** I pray that you will continually experience the immeasurable greatness of God's power made available to you through faith. **Then your lives will be an advertisement of this immense power as it works through you! This is the mighty power 20** that was released when God raised Christ from the dead and exalted him to the place of highest honor and supreme authority in the heavenly realm! **21** And now he is exalted as first above every ruler, authority, government, and realm of power in existence! He is gloriously enthroned over every name that is ever praised, not only in this age, but in the age that is coming! (Ephesians 1:18-21, TPT)

This is a power packed set of scriptures. I hope that the eyes of your imagination be opened until you experience the wealth of God's glorious inheritances that he finds in us. It is ours to experience, but we have to know that we can experience it all now. We are one In Christ. We are completely unified with the Father therefore our experiences to this point in history don't stack up to his example. Which leads us to the other part of unity, which is being unified with each other.

When one part of the body suffers, we all suffer. Compassion is awesome, pity isn't. Compassion has power. Pity is pathetic. Yet, time after time we'll see leaders simply place a hand on a sick member in an act of pious pity. This is where our imagination should set in, it opens us up to the supernatural things of God. Our imagination creates hope (confident expectation), and allows us to experience what is possible, it opens our hearts up to what was seemingly impossible before.

Then in verse nineteen, Paul starts talking about the immeasurable greatness of God's power made available. He is talking about while we are alive on earth. Because it states how our lives will be an advertisement of this immense power as it works through you. Folks, we aren't simply talking about "a sinner's prayer" here. We are talking about changed lives walking in immense power. This is what we get when we know of our oneness with The Father and Son. Even further, the more unified the body of believers are, the greater the experience of what is truly possible with God. Unity creates harmony which in turn results in greater experiences. The problem has been that prior to about 100 years ago, the body of Christ has been inside four walls huddled together instead of representing a force of good to be reckoned with. We've been a social club complaining how wicked the world is. Yet, we've done nothing to show the world the power of Christ working through us. We've had a resemblance of unity by being just as sick and diseased as the "world" surrounding the four walls and just as reliant on medicine as "worldly people." In the first century church, there was a boldness and unity even under extreme persecution. Yet, they were gentle as lambs towards unbelievers showing them the way to salvation. This was through using the power of Christ within them.

They weren't picketing abortion clinics nor were exclaiming how God would send them all to hell. They were showing the true power and authority we have In Christ. The unity is in the power of God through his sons and daughters making a gentle, but powerful stand towards ministering to others. It is not in saying "Come, Lord Jesus. destroy all the wicked and evil people on this Earth." It is embracing those "sinners" and blanketing them in power and love. The unity of standing for the sinner is powerful itself. Making a stand against atheists isn't the gospel of love. In meekness and humility, showing the power of Christ is what makes a difference.

Imagine this: every Christian walking in divine health, divine prosperity, and divine love. This is a part of being in union (unity) with Christ. It isn't separate, and as more believers are walking in the truest form of God's Kingdom on Earth, the more people will be added into the Kingdom on this Earth. The Kingdom of God is the most powerful and the only true kingdom, we're part of it. The Creator himself has made Jesus King of his kingdom, and we carry the kingdom wherever we go. If there is no Name higher than Christ, then that means all things must submit to us. We should be proudly bearing the banner of the Kingdom of God, by our actions performed in Love and Power.

On Veterans Day of this year (2019), I went to a restaurant for my free meal. The restaurant had a patio, so I decided to enjoy my juicy steak there. Another veteran saw me sitting outside in thirty-degree weather and decided to join me. He asked about my blue hair, which I began to give my testimony on how Jesus healed me of Lou Gehrig's disease. Blue is the prophetic color of healing, I stated. He began to give me a list of his medical problems, most of them stemming from his time in Vietnam. I simply said, "Well, you're as healed as I am. Now just jump up outta that chair!" He did and said he felt a huge change. He also told me of his wife's medical problems, to which I stated that she's healed as well. We parted ways as he stated how glad he was that he had come out to the patio. I didn't even mention that I'd been on my phone when he first showed up. The phone call was about a three-thousand-dollar bill that I didn't owe. This was an important phone call. Yet, I discerned the need to hang up on the customer service representative to talk to this fella. That's living and being a part of God's Kingdom. When I called back, the customer service representative had already cleared the matter up. Thank you, Jesus.

Wednesday, I was delivering coffee to a church. There was a man working there, but the pastor wasn't there. Since my arms were full, I just walked into the church and set the coffee down on the nearest table. We talked about an hour, then I left. I, later, called the Pastor. He stated that he had been trying to get this man to church for about seven months and he didn't know what I said to this man, but that it had a profound effect on him. I don't know what I said either, but you can bet it's the Holy Spirit working on him.

These are just a few examples of how we should be living in God's Kingdom. Every day as I'm out and about doing the things that I need to do, there's at least one person that has a need to be met. Friday I was getting new tires for my vehicle, there was another couple waiting for their car to be fixed. The woman said how much she loved my blue hair, which I gave my testimony, and then prayed for their health problems. None of this happens without a renewing of the mind, knowing that we're unified in Christ. It doesn't happen by thinking the Kingdom of God is somewhere out there and we're waiting for it to come down.

My computer went down, I had planned to miss that day's church service to continue working on this book. Because I couldn't work on the book, I went on to the service. There were about thirty people present. Pastor decided to make it a healing service and he asked me to pray for those who needed healing. Every person with the exception of one was healed. The next day, my computer started working properly. I'm always in God's Kingdom, so I am always operating in it wherever I may be. This is the mindset we should all be in. This is not including the phone calls that come in from all over the world. Sometimes, I'm giving the gift of knowledge, and other times a prophetic word. Still other times, I'm offering a word of wisdom, gift of healing, or whatever that person needs. Jesus told us the parable of the mustard seed.

> **31** It is like a mustard seed planted in the ground. It is the smallest of all seeds, **32** but it becomes the largest of all garden plants; it grows long branches, and birds can make nests in its shade." (Mark 4:31-32, NLT)

The seed was Jesus. He was the bearer of the seed of the Kingdom of God. He was planted in the ground, then arose. The Kingdom of God started out with one small seed, Christ Jesus. It was the smallest kingdom until his resurrection. Then for forty years that seed was watered, fed, and persecuted. It then became a tree, and endured much persecution by the human established kingdom of the religious minded Jewish leadership and by the Roman Government. Those human governments were overthrown in 70 A.D. From that moment forward, that mustard seed became a tree and largest and only true kingdom on the Earth. This is also what Jesus meant when he stated that.

> **12** And from the time John the Baptist began preaching until now, the Kingdom of Heaven has been forcefully advancing, and violent people are attacking it. **13** For before John came, all the prophets and the law of Moses looked forward to this present time. **14** And if you are willing to accept what I say, he is Elijah, the one the prophets said would come. (Matthew 11:12-14, NLT)

There was that period of forty years, where the Kingdom of Heaven/ God was attacked to the point of scarcely surviving. Now it has grown to the largest Kingdom on Earth. Yet, we still view God's Kingdom as having yet to be established. It is established and is the ruling authority. We now have to learn that and to start walking in all the power that a ruling kingdom has. When we know we're unified with the King, then we start walking in that power that is available to us now, knowing our needs are met, and sharing that with others. That is renewing our minds to what is available right now. We aren't walking in that, because we think it's a transparent kingdom awaiting to come. Therefore, we think we are still subject to the physical authorities on this Earth, and while we obey the laws of the land, we are not subject to them for our abundant life. Rather, we are subjects of the King Jesus with whom we are in unity and with whom we have our inheritance. We are no longer subjects to the physical nature of things if we would only believe that the Kingdom is now.

The thing is that people are still looking for a human mouthpiece in the form of a human leader. The five-fold ministry isn't and never was made to be a substitute for Christ, rather to lead you to relying on Holy Spirit, not on another human being. In this walk, I've seen time and time, people running from spiritual leader to leader. It's because we're placing our trust in another human being not in God.

> **34** And they will not need to teach their neighbors, nor will they need to teach their relatives, saying, 'You should know the Lord.' For everyone, from the least to the greatest, will know me already," says the Lord. "And I will forgive their wickedness, and I will never again remember their sins." (Jeremiah 31:34, NLT)

Understand this; when a New Testament writer references a scripture from a prophet, it's because that scripture is fulfilled at that time.

> **11** And the result of this will be that everyone will know me as Lord! There will be no need at all to teach their fellow-citizens or brothers by saying, 'You should know the Lord Jehovah,' since everyone will know me inwardly, from the most unlikely to the most distinguished. (Hebrews 8:11, TPT)

Quit putting human leaders on a pedestal they don't belong on. The Holy Spirit does use the five-fold ministry, but each of you is to be led inwardly by the Holy Spirit. We are simply the nudge to gently guide you in the right direction. There should come a time when your primary teacher isn't a human being. That is, when you become part of the five-fold ministry leading others to be reliant on Holy Spirit. Yes, we are all supposed to be a part of the five-fold because this isn't a human appointed position, but a spirit appointed one. And it isn't a church appointed position as we make it out to be. The more we place our focus on being spirit led, the less we'll need human leaders. Then no matter our walk-in life, we become the sent one, worker of miracles, teacher, etc., until we are all guided by the Holy Spirit in the fullness of Christ.

Living a supernatural lifestyle also means being unified one with the Father, Jesus and Holy Spirit which will lead to a unified body of Christ where each member is equal and all are servants of each other. When all are operating in unity, there is no need for "gifts." All will be operating full-time in the supernatural fullness of Christ. Each and every need will be met by the Holy Spirit within us. There will be no need to "impart" a gift to another believer. This is what the church should be working towards. Every person becoming Spirit efficient, not reliant upon another human being. The government of the Kingdom isn't a pyramid, or a government organized like the United States. There is one monarch. Yes, absolutely. That is Jesus. But every single person has direct access to The King. It doesn't go from the King to one or two treasured office holders then filtering down to other offices until it reaches the "commoners." No, each one of us has direct connection to the King who is Lord of all, with no one family member having something the others don't have:

> **6** And you will be my kingdom of priests, my holy nation.' This is the message you must give to the people of Israel." (Exodus 19:6, NLT) **17** Moses led them out from the camp to meet with God, and they stood at the foot of the mountain. (Exodus 19:17, NLT)

The Father's intention was that all of Israel would be one with Him. He, at first, gave the commandments to all of Israel. He came down to meet with them all personally. They refused, instead having Moses substitute in for them, which is why it is called the Law of Moses.

> **5** and from Jesus Christ. He is the faithful witness to these things, the first to rise from the dead, and the ruler of all the kings of the world. All glory to him who loves us and has freed us from our sins by shedding his blood for us. **6** He has made us a Kingdom of priests for God his Father. All glory and power to him forever and ever! Amen. (Revelation 1:5-6, NLT)

In God's Kingdom we are all equals, because His Spirit dwells in all of us. No one person is above another. Rather, we are all Kings and Priests, a sanctified and Holy Nation under Christ. Understand this concept of being unified, then you shall see that you are as capable as anyone of walking in a supernatural lifestyle being whole and complete as a true son or daughter.

Worksheet: Chapter 10

1. Describe the definition of Unity.

____
____
____
____

2. What is the actuality of being unified, as defined in this chapter?

____
____
____
____

3. If we are all unified In Christ, then is one person above another? Or does one person have something that another one doesn't have?

____
____
____
____

4. Do we all have a direct connection with the Father?

____
____

5. If as He is, so are we in this world, (see 1 John 4:17) then are we not all equal In Christ?

____
____

11. The truest form of Giving

There is no step by step list of how to walk in the supernatural in your everyday life. The basic formula is the same as discussed in 'Unlocking the Mystery of Divine Healing'. Believe that all your needs are met and expect there to be changes. Once again, belief plus expectation equals your needs met. Take the limitations out of your life. We place the limits on how much the Holy Spirit can work in our personal lives.

When you take a long look at the Gospels, Jesus cared about the physical lives of those who came into contact with Him. There is more talk about the physical life, than about after our physical life. There are teachings how we're supposed to suffer and experience lack in order to serve Jesus. That isn't what he shows us. We are supposed to enjoy this life and spread that enjoyment to others:

> **9** For you have experienced the extravagant grace of our Lord Jesus Christ, that although he was infinitely rich, he impoverished himself for our sake, so that by his poverty, we could become rich beyond measure. (2 Corinthians 8:9, TPT)

There are many scriptures supporting that believers of Christ should not be lacking in any way. God the Loving Father wants to supply all our needs and it's his good pleasure to provide for us. In the Old Testament, we see that those who served God were indeed immensely blessed. Everyone from Abraham down to King Solomon were all blessed. Joseph was the second most powerful man in all of Egypt. Each one of Jacob's sons were all blessed, King David was blessed. Moses was blessed, it would indeed be hard to find one servant of God that wasn't blessed. Job was blessed prior to his affliction and afterwards even more blessed. I refer back to my statement earlier we are in the most powerful Kingdom, so therefore all of its citizens should be blessed. Do not despise the riches of the Kingdom of God.

The New Testament is no different, let's take a look at some supporting scriptures.

> **24** Until now you've not been bold enough to ask the Father for a single thing in my name, but now you can ask, and keep on asking him! And you can be sure that you'll receive what you ask for, and your joy will have no limits! (John 16:24, TPT)

> **10** A thief has only one thing in mind—he wants to steal, slaughter, and destroy. But I have come to give you everything in abundance, more than you expect—life in its fullness until you overflow! (John 10:10, TPT)

Joy without limits, life in its fullness to overflowing. This doesn't sound like a Father who wants his kids to be in lack and suffering. Those words are in red, so they come directly from our king. Let's go back up to John 16:24, just because I know the mindset of people. Where it states to ask and keep on asking him, in other words have a huge list! This isn't begging him until you receive that one thing you're asking for, not in the least. This means to ask him for any and everything and the answer is already yes. We don't have to beg and plead with God until we've begged and pleaded enough to where the Father says, "Ok, you've twisted my arm enough. I'll grudgingly give it to you." That word ask actually means to seize it, take a hold of it. This scripture is stating that it yours already:

> **6** And without faith living within us it would be impossible to please God. For we come to God in faith knowing that he is real and that he rewards the faith of those who give all their passion and strength into seeking him. (Hebrews 11:6, TPT)

This translation of this verse is the best, without faith living within us. We as believers have faith living within. He is the spirit of faith the Holy Spirit. He rewards those who believe and seek him. This is lavishly. He doesn't hold back, now if we only start truly believing this.

> **18–19** Then you will be empowered to discover what every holy one experiences—the great magnitude of the astonishing love of Christ in all its dimensions. How deeply intimate and far-reaching is his love! How enduring and inclusive it is! Endless love beyond measurement that transcends our understanding—this extravagant love pours into you until you are filled to overflowing with the fullness of God! **20** Never doubt God's mighty power to work in you and accomplish all this. He will achieve infinitely more than your greatest request, your most unbelievable dream,

> and exceed your wildest imagination! He will outdo them all, for his miraculous power constantly energizes you. (Ephesians 3:18-20, TPT)

The Heavenly Father has no lack. Neither wants us to live in lack. It takes us simply believing that. He gives freely to us and these supporting scriptures are all over the bible. He is a Father of abundance. This is in all areas of our lives. Seeking 'first the Kingdom of God' is relying on the Father to provide for his children's needs. Jesus tells us how the birds do not worry because they are provided for. The flowers of the field don't work or toil but are clothed splendidly. All provided for by The Father. It is all provided for without stress, strife or worry. How much more will the Father provide for us? The problem is we try to seek them out for ourselves instead of letting the heavenly Father provide for us. When we know that our righteousness is in Christ, we can then start trusting God to supernaturally provide these things for us. As the below scripture states, "then all these less important things will be given to you abundantly:"

> **33** "So above all, constantly chase after the realm of God's kingdom and the righteousness that proceeds from him. Then all these less important things will be given to you abundantly. **34** Refuse to worry about tomorrow, but deal with each challenge that comes your way, one day at a time. Tomorrow will take care of itself." (Matthew 6:33-34, TPT)

Notice in the following three verses this applies to this lifetime right now:

> **8** Yes, God is more than ready to overwhelm you with every form of grace, so that you will have more than enough of everything —every moment and in every way. He will make you overflow with abundance in every good thing you do. (2 Corinthians 9:8, TPT)

> **17** Every gift God freely gives us is good and perfect, streaming down from the Father of lights, who shines from the heavens with no hidden shadow or darkness and is never subject to change. (James 1:17, TPT)

> **19** I am convinced that my God will fully satisfy every need you have, for I have seen the abundant riches of glory revealed to me through the Anointed One, Jesus Christ! (Philippians 4:19, TPT)

The only condition is coming to know you are his righteousness. Quit trying to get these things by your own manipulation. Acquire them supernaturally by trusting that it is His good pleasure to provide these things for you. Quit chasing after them. Instead, know he will supernaturally cancel debts and provide for you with an abundance. When God supernaturally provides for you, it isn't at anyone else's expense. Then it is from your abundance you can selflessly provide for others. Where one is blessed in God's Kingdom, all should be blessed. Since we know all our needs are provided for, we can lavishly bless those that have needs.

This isn't giving to get, nor is it giving out of obligation. It is giving because your needs are already met. Therefore, the giving comes out of the love shed abroad in your heart by the Holy Spirit (see Romans 5:5). We are fixing to discuss some ways the church manipulates and hurts the true message of what we have in Christ. But first here's a huge scripture that will show a number of things:

> **8** I'm not saying this as though I were issuing an order but to stir you to greater love by mentioning the enthusiasm of the Macedonians as a challenge to you. 9 For you have experienced the extravagant grace of our Lord Jesus Christ, that although he was infinitely rich, he impoverished himself for our sake, so that by his poverty, we could become rich beyond measure.

> **10** So here are my thoughts concerning this matter, and it's in your best interests. Since you made such a good start last year, both in the grace of giving and in your longing to give, **11** you should finish what you started. You were so eager in your intentions to give, so go do it. Finish this act of worship according to your ability to give. **12** For if the intention and desire are there, the size of the gift doesn't matter. Your gift is fully acceptable to God according to what you have, not what you don't have. **13** I'm not saying this in order to ease someone else's load by overloading you, but as a matter of fair balance. **14** Your surplus could meet their need, and their abundance may one day meet your need. This equal sharing of abundance will mean a fair balance. **15** As it is written: the one who gathered much didn't have too much, and the one who gathered little didn't have too little. (2 Corinthians 8:8-15, TPT)

Paul wasn't issuing an order. He was encouraging the Corinthians based upon their previous desire to help. He stresses to give according to their ability to give, not to overburden themselves and do without. He is talking about giving from their surplus as a matter of fair balance. This isn't giving to get, for the Lord's desire is to meet the needs of all. He pours everything out freely by his abundance of grace. Grace meaning God's ability to do that which a man cannot do. In other words, supernaturally being provided for. The Corinthians were flourishing based upon their faith in God to provide for them. The others at this time were lacking in seeing their fruit of faith. Therefore, Paul was encouraging them to give until such a time the others faith caught up with them and they could trust God to provide for them. That all needs were met. This is the fair balance so that all have more than enough. This is how God's Kingdom works.

Now notice in the above verses how there are three things not expressed by Paul.

1. Giving to receive (blessing to be blessed).

2. A veiled threat that if they didn't give, they wouldn't be blessed.

3. That they were under an obligation to give.

Firstly, do you realize that the Temple of Jerusalem wasn't built from taking away from those who lacked? The Temple of Jerusalem was built from supernatural surplus and from the riches of Solomon, which the Lord God had given unto him. It wasn't built from lack or causing a debt to the nation of Israel. Yet, from the pulpit and other ministries *it is taught to give until it hurts*. If you are in lack, give from the lack to receive. *That is so unscriptural.* Hold on one moment I so need some coffee!

Here come the words that cause so much division in the body of Christ, The Tithe. If you're a pastor or have a ministry you just took a deep breath and just accused me of not wanting to give. The way the tithe is taught is not biblical at all, it is a means of the business called "Church" to tax and manipulate those who profess to be Christians. If a church or ministry is teaching that you are obligated to give or give to get, then on this topic they are outside of God's Truth and not teaching scriptures correctly. They are not trusting in God. Rather, they are relying on human wisdom to stay in business and to gain profit. Those who use the 501(c)(3) in order to encourage giving are in truth. Using a human system to get its members to contribute to its organization what's that called? It's called blackmail or bribery, that is what it is (give to get). In fact, they are asking you to use your faith to give without having the faith for themselves that God will provide for them. Instead they are using manipulation to get their needs met, this is not Godly.

Please notice I didn't say 501(c)(3) is ungodly, it is a good and much needed thing. It is the motivation or manipulation by some leaders that is wrong. If the only reason members give is for a tax break, they are wrong as well.

We have first fruits that Cain and Abel gave. This was not out of obligation but was from gratitude to God. It didn't cause Cain or Abel hardship in anyway whatsoever. With Cain however on one occasion God wasn't pleased with that offering, because of a wrong heart motivation, which I'm not going to try to speculate on. Then we get to Abraham:

> **17** After Abram returned from his victory over Kedorlaomer and all his allies, the king of Sodom went out to meet him in the valley of Shaveh (that is, the King's Valley).**18** And Melchizedek, the king of Salem and a priest of God Most High, brought Abram some bread and wine. **19** Melchizedek blessed Abram with this blessing: "Blessed be Abram by God Most High, Creator of heaven and earth. **20** And blessed be God Most High, who has defeated your enemies for you." **Then Abram gave Melchizedek a tenth of all the goods he had recovered. 21** The king of Sodom said to Abram, "Give back my people who were captured. But you may keep for yourself all the goods you have recovered." **22** Abram replied to the king of Sodom, "I solemnly swear to the Lord, God Most High, Creator of heaven and earth, **23** that I will not take so much as a single thread or sandal thong from what belongs to you. **Otherwise you might say, 'I am the one who made Abram rich.' 24** I will accept only what my young warriors have already eaten, **and I request that you give a fair share of the goods to my allies**—Aner, Eshcol, and Mamre." (Genesis 14:17-24, NLT)

Abraham gave to Melchizedek from the goods that he had recovered. He did this willingly without an obligation to do so as an act of honor. Then, he gave to the king of Sodom what he was asking for so that his allies be given a fair share because of their alliance. The reason Abraham gave is quite clear: because Abraham wouldn't allow them to have room to say that they made him rich. His prosperity came from God. Abraham wasn't giving from his own personal abundance. Rather, he was simply giving back what had previously belonged to others. So, to speculate that this was out of obligation and therefore it is a tithe is not scriptural. It was done prior to the Law of Moses.

> **13** At the top of the stairway stood the Lord, and he said, "I am the Lord, the God of your grandfather Abraham, and the God of your father, Isaac. The ground you are lying on belongs to you. I am giving it to you and your descendants. (Genesis 28:13, NLT)

> **22** And this memorial pillar I have set up will become a place for worshiping God, and I will present to God a tenth of everything he gives me." (Genesis 28:22, NLT)

This set the boundaries up for the tithe promised by Jacob which was the land given to Jacob and to his descendants. There was no tithe for those that lived outside the boundaries of the nation of Israel. The tithe was only in place for descendants of Jacob and were only things that came directly from the land of Israel: grains, fruits, oils, spices, and animals that grazed from the land. Money was never a tithe.

> **30** "One-tenth of the produce of the land, whether grain from the fields or fruit from the trees, belongs to the Lord and must be set apart to him as holy. **31** If you want to buy back the Lord's tenth of the grain or fruit, you must pay its value, plus 20 percent. **32** Count off every tenth animal from

> your herds and flocks and set them apart for the Lord as holy. (Leviticus 27:30-32, NLT)

Under the Law of Moses there were three types of tithes set up. The first was general tithe which was given to the Levitical Priesthood for their service to the tabernacle. They were not given the land inheritance. So, it was for their personal consumption. They still had to tithe a tenth of that:

> **21** As for the tribe of Levi, your relatives, I will compensate them for their service in the Tabernacle. Instead of an allotment of land, I will give them the tithes from the entire land of Israel. **22** "From now on, no Israelites except priests or Levites may approach the Tabernacle. If they come too near, they will be judged guilty and will die. **23** Only the Levites may serve at the Tabernacle, and they will be held responsible for any offenses against it. This is a permanent law for you, to be observed from generation to generation. The Levites will receive no allotment of land among the Israelites, **24** because I have given them the Israelites' tithes, which have been presented as sacred offerings to the Lord. This will be the Levites' share. That is why I said they would receive no allotment of land among the Israelites." **25** The Lord also told Moses, **26** "Give these instructions to the Levites: When you receive from the people of Israel the tithes I have assigned as your allotment, give a tenth of the tithes you receive—a tithe of the tithe—to the Lord as a sacred offering.(Numbers 18:21-26, NLT)

The second, **tithe of worship**, is the second type of tithe which, once again, were only things consumed off of the land of Israel. This was consumed by the tither in a designated place. If that place was far away, then it would be changed into money. Once the destination was reached, the money was then used to buy the tithe back for it to be consumed by the tither.

> **22** "You must set aside a tithe of your crops—one-tenth of all the crops you harvest each year. **23** Bring this tithe to the designated place of worship—the place the Lord your God chooses for his name to be honored—and eat it there in his presence. This applies to your tithes of grain, new wine, olive oil, and the firstborn males of your flocks and herds. Doing this will teach you always to fear the Lord your God. **24** "Now when the Lord your God blesses you with a good harvest, the place of worship he chooses for his name to be honored might be too far for you to bring the tithe. **25** If so, you may sell the tithe portion of your crops and herds, put the money in a pouch, and go to the place the Lord your God has chosen. **26** When you arrive, you may use the money to buy any kind of food you want—cattle, sheep, goats, wine, or other alcoholic drink. Then feast there in the presence of the Lord your God and celebrate with your household. **27** And do not neglect the Levites in your town, for they will receive no allotment of land among you. (Deuteronomy 14:22-27, NLT)

The third tithe is the **welfare tithe**. This was to be given every three years and provided to the local area for the feeding of the local Levites, the widow, orphans and the strangers living among the children of Israel. These strangers were not under a tithe at all since the tithe was only imposed on the children of Jacob (Israel).

> **28** "At the end of every third year, **bring the entire tithe of that year's harvest** and store it in the nearest town. **29** Give it to the Levites, who will receive no allotment of land among you, as well as to the foreigners living among you, the orphans, and the widows in your towns, **so they can eat and be satisfied.** Then the Lord your God will bless you in all your work. (Deuteronomy 14: 28-29, NLT)

As you see, the tithe was set up so that none would go hungry. This is not even remotely transferable to the Christian churches of today. You cannot even be obligated to tithe if you are not a descendant of Jacob living in the land given by God to Jacob and his descendants. The disciples who were with Jesus were not obligated to tithe since they were fisherman and fish wasn't under the law of tithing, because fish do not live on the land allotted to Jacob. Jesus did not pay a tithe either. Oh, and did you notice that the welfare tithe was only every three years and only for that year's harvest not a combination of all three years? Also notable is that in the third year, there wasn't a worship tithe or a general tithe. All of that year's tithe went to the welfare tithe.

Now for the blame game that most churches use, the Book of Malachi. Stating that you are robbing God for not tithing is easily put to rest. The book of Malachi is directed to the Levites. Yes, the entire book. It is not directed towards any other person. It was the priesthood themselves who were robbing God, not the common person. So, I'm sorry if your local leadership is pointing the finger at you for not paying the tithe. Then, point the finger right back at them because if you're going to transfer the tithe of the Old Covenant to New Covenant believers, then the Levitical Priesthood transfers to the leaders of your local church. Therefore, they are the ones robbing from God!

> **6** The Lord of Heaven's Armies says to the priests…. (Malachi 1:6, NLT)
>
> **1** "Listen, you priests—this command is for you! 2 Listen to me and make up your minds to honor my name," says the Lord of Heaven's Armies, "or I will bring a terrible curse against you. I will curse even the blessings you receive. (Malachi 2:1-2, NLT)

> **2** .... For he will be like a blazing fire that refines metal, or like a strong soap that bleaches clothes. **3** He will sit like a refiner of silver, burning away the dross. He will purify the Levites, refining them like gold and silver, so that they may once again offer acceptable sacrifices to the Lord. (Malachi 3:2-3, NLT)

The Levitical Priesthood was taking the tithe and offering, and selling them, then replacing them with defective replacements. They were then pocketing the difference in money.

> **8** When you give blind animals as sacrifices, isn't that wrong? And isn't it wrong to offer animals that are crippled and diseased? Try giving gifts like that to your governor, and see how pleased he is!" says the Lord of Heaven's Armies. (Malachi 1:8, NLT)

We should absolutely give to our local churches and ministries that teach truthfully about the tithe, teaching that you are not obligated to give. We should give and give abundantly from our surplus, absolutely! If there is a ministry that has sown selflessly, give to that ministry or church as abundantly as you are able. Be a cheerful giver and give without hesitation, because of the blessings the Lord has given unto you freely!

> **18** For the Scriptures have taught us: "Do not muzzle an ox or forbid it to eat while it grinds the grain." And also, "The one who labors deserves his wages." (1 Timothy 5:18, TPT)

> **7** Let giving flow from your heart, not from a sense of religious duty. Let it spring up freely from the joy of giving—all because God loves hilarious generosity! (2 Corinthians 9:7, TPT)

When we are blessed, we should share that blessing. When we have a need, that need should be filled. Let us all walk in the faithfulness of Our Father and be quick to give and share our blessings. There should not be a need in the body of Christ that is not met. We should all be very quick and faithful to give to those less fortunate while they learn to have their needs met by our faithful, never changing Father.

Worksheet: Chapter 11

1. Why should we give?

2. Where should we be giving from, lack or from being blessed?

3. Will the Father provide supernatural provision? Give an example of a supernatural provision you received.

4. Should you feel condemned if you can't give? Give a reason why or why not.

5. What were the three types of tithe and give an explanation of why they were put in place?

6. The whole book of Malachi is directed towards whom?

7. Does God want us to live an abundant life, is it his pleasure to supernaturally provide for us?

NOTES:

12. Love and Intimacy as children

> **13** Until then, there are three things that remain: faith, hope, and love—yet love surpasses them all. So above all else, let love be the beautiful prize for which you run. (1 Corinthians 13:13, TPT)

Everything springs forth from love. Knowing the love of the Father is where faith and hope (confident expectation) springs forth. Likewise, it is from love that the supernatural flows. We spend far too much time arguing theology and not enough time pondering the Father's love. When we know of the Father's love for us, that is when faith which is trust and confident expectation wells up inside and flows outwardly. The end result is then the supernatural. When the full revelation of the Love of The Father is revealed to us, we then trust in Him that all of our needs are met. Then, when we have a need, the right words just flow out and our

God-fueled expectation overwhelms the negative circumstances and the miraculous is born.

> **5** And this hope is not a disappointing fantasy, because we can now experience the endless love of God cascading into our hearts through the Holy Spirit who lives in us! (Romans 5:5, TPT)

Love is not the result of what we do, rather it is placed into us by the Holy Spirit. Then our actions reflect that which was already planted inside of us. Where does peace that surpasses all understanding come from? Peace comes from the love placed inside of us. Religious Christianity is born from trying to achieve what has been inside of us all along. Striving comes from trying to get something we already have. Instead of having we are trying to achieve. We base our achievements by our actions and judge others based on this false premise, which leads to a critical judging heart. We haven't attained perfection, so we require this perfection from others. Then, in order to feel that we have attained perfection, we make a list of do's and don'ts. The end result is a never-ending list of rules that lead to frustration and judgment towards others. All of this blocks the flow of the supernatural, because it is not based upon the love of Christ, but on our actions. Christ frees us from this internal struggle. Everything we need is already placed inside of us. There is no more trying to prove ourselves. That is when what is already in us flows outward.

We as believers should have more inner peace than any other people group. Yet, we are for the most part the most stressed, and anxious people group there is. It is because we have this long list of things we have to do and even a longer list of what not to do, all of this is based upon appearances. Most spend their lives trying to complete these lists based upon outside appearances. Fear, anxiety and worry all block the supernatural, because it isn't based on love, or faith. Fear comes from needs not being met, or the thinking that our needs won't be met, so then we have to come up with the solution on our own. It is also always based on outside circumstances, so how can the supernatural happen when the supernatural flows from knowing our needs are met. Few believers achieve peace, because they feel that they have the burden of the whole world upon them and even attaining heaven is based on their actions. We can have supernatural peace, because it isn't based on your actions, nor on the physical circumstances.

> **6** Don't be pulled in different directions or worried about a thing. Be saturated in prayer throughout each day, offering your faith-filled requests before God **with overflowing gratitude. Tell him every detail of your life, 7 then God's wonderful peace that transcends human understanding**, will make the answers known to you through Jesus Christ. **8** So keep your thoughts continually fixed on all that is authentic and real, honorable and admirable, beautiful and respectful, pure and holy, merciful and kind. **And fasten your thoughts on every glorious work of God, praising him always. 9** Follow the example of all that we have imparted to you and the God of peace will be with you in all things. (Philippians 4:6-9, TPT)

The answer is to include God the Father in your daily life, knowing you are one with Him. He is literally with you, because you are His temple. Gratitude comes from knowing that needs are met. Quit thinking that God is somewhere out there. He is in you, and when you make him a part of your daily life then you will be at peace in all situations and you will have the answers you need with every circumstance. They will just flow out of you, without having to think about it, because internally He is supplying the answers to you. Let's talk about prayer, it's simply communication and it doesn't have to be in words. It is simply awareness and knowing He is within you. Many people look for God to speak to them in only three ways:

1. Through other people (verbal language) and sometimes through an audible voice.

2. Through Scriptures.

3. Through emotions/feelings.

Since the Holy Spirit is in you, He doesn't need to use verbal communication. Nor does He have to use emotions. He does use these three ways, but they are just starting points. Depending on how a person is taught most primarily will use only one of these three ways more regularly. The majority of people in my opinion think that the only way the Father communicates is through scripture and even then, only through scripture through a preacher or religious figure. Then there is the other side which is primarily through emotions/feelings. These three ways are only superficial which should lead to a deeper form of communication that needs no words or feelings. Let's call this spiritual extrasensory perception (esp). The end result of it can come out as words, feelings, or things that some people would translate as manifestations of the Holy Spirit. Yet, it's starting point is deep within and just a knowing that you know and you can't even put a description on it. Then it bubbles to the surface as words, feelings, or even visions. I'm quite sure everyone of us have had these experiences, but we're often too focused on external things to recognize it. Our thoughts are just too busy swirling around in our head. We're rationalizing things out through verbal language in our head, so we totally miss out on the spiritual esp. It often surprises people when they propose something to me and then state, "take time to pray about it", the majority of time I already have the answer, my response is often I already did and here's my answer. It doesn't take hours, days, months or years to hear from God. That's in the Old Testament, prior to us having direct access to Our Father. Jesus had the answers to everything immediately, and I don't recall even one-time Jesus stated "hold on a second, I have to talk to my Father". He knew because he was one with the Holy Spirit, as we are now. Our idea of prayer is so outta whack.

We think of prayer as being on our knees with our hands folded together. Yet, we should be in constant communication with the Holy Spirit. Whether we're driving, working, shopping or visiting with a friend. It doesn't even have to look weird or strange, because it is internally. I really want to impart to you a step by step process to achieve this, but there are dangers if I do, and they are already taught by other people. The problem is that either it turns into a religious practice and the result is no change or intimacy, or it becomes a weirded-out practice leading to a whole bunch of craziness. Really it comes down to an awareness and that awareness will lead you into what works for you. It is after *all a personal relationship*! I really believe this is why Paul writes: *"So keep your thoughts continually fixed on all that is authentic and real, honorable and admirable, beautiful and respectful, pure and holy, merciful and kind.* **And fasten your thoughts on every glorious work of God, praising him always.**" When we keep our thoughts on those things, that will lead into a personal relationship. Notice the special emphasis: "*on every glorious work of God, praising him always*". This isn't praising him for the troubles of life, but for the blessings. He isn't the cause of the troubles of this life, he's the solution.

> **17** Every gift God freely gives us is good and perfect, streaming down from the Father of lights, who shines from the heavens with no hidden shadow or darkness and is never subject to change. (James 1:17, TPT)

What is coming up now is guidance on how to have such a personal relationship that we no longer need verbal language to know what Holy Spirit is saying.

1. Study the Bible for yourself, don't depend on someone else's interpretation, look past the words.

2. Use your imagination.

3. Speak in tongues often.

4. Quiet time- without using words, quiet your thoughts.

5. Act impulsively to help another person.

Study for yourself

I believe in studying scriptures, it's a starting point to come to a relationship with the Holy Spirit, the Father and Jesus.

> **16** Every Scripture has been written by the Holy Spirit, the breath of God. It will empower you by its instruction and correction, giving you the strength to take the right direction and lead you deeper into the path of godliness. **17** Then you will be God's servant, fully mature and perfectly prepared to fulfill any assignment God gives you. (2 Timothy 3:16-17, TPT)

Here's the key to this verse *leading you deeper into the path of godliness.* Our relationship with God doesn't start and end with scriptures. Paul himself was referring to the Torah, he was a master scholar and knew these scriptures in-depth. Yet, until the road to Damascus, there was no relationship. This was a person that had direct access to the Torah, written in his own language. He also knew all of the customs of the day intimately. Yet, he was gone astray without relationship until he had his own experience. We can spend forty years studying the words without ever having a truly personal relationship. A person such as Paul was sincere, but was led astray out of ignorance, because the written words were all he knew. He, until Damascus, lived from the written words taking a hard-line stance on them.

When I first started studying scriptures it was without a human being teaching me their interpretation. Thank you, Jesus! Where other people just look at words on a page, and come to a hardnosed interpretation, I let Holy Spirit show me the meaning behind the words. Letting the verse addresses disappear along with the chapter separations I read the New Testament as it were. They were letters, so follow the whole line of thought not just one sentence. We take so much out of context based upon the slant of how we perceive scriptures. We rip one scripture out and then base our perception on that one scripture. It's all because man assigned a number to a sentence or group of sentences. If we did that to any book, then that book would make no sense and the author's points would be completely missed. That's what happens with the bible. We don't even take into account the who, what, when and where. When we teach reading comprehension, we're taught to look at who is speaking, who they are speaking to, what is the discussion is about, what is the main topic, when was it written and what were the circumstances around the main thought. When it comes to scripture very few people use this formula. Very few people ever think about the culture of the people of that day. It was completely different.

It gets worse when people use scriptures from the Old Testament, using a scripture and saying, "God said", well guess what? Three quarters of the time it wasn't God saying it. Then you have people taking the Old Covenant and sticking it right into the New Covenant even though they are completely different covenants. The Old Covenant was between God and a person, Moses, representing the whole nation of Israel with the high priest being from the lineage of Aaron, who was the first high priest. In the

New Covenant it's between God and His Son Christ Jesus, we aren't involved in it. Which is why we have to accept Christ to be included in it. With our High Priest being Jesus not after the order of Aaron, but after the order of Melchizedek. My point being look at scriptures with fresh eyes and an open heart, then you will see a perspective of God that most people do not get from the pulpit of religion.

Use your imagination:

That's right, you have a God given imagination for a purpose. Yes, there is vain imagination and I caution against that. I am talking about Godly imagination guided by the Holy Spirit. There are three different ways to use your imagination in a Godly way.

1. While reading scriptures.

2. Imagine the Holy Spirit inside of yourself.

3. Imagine yourself doing supernatural works.

While reading scriptures. Imagine yourself as actually being a part of what you're reading about. You can apply this to the Gospels, the book of Acts and the Old Testament. This itself will push the boundaries of your thoughts. This will open your thoughts to the impossible. The way the brain works, it stores the memory of the imagination as if you truly did experience it. The brain doesn't know the difference between the imagination or actually experiencing something in reality. While reading the letters in the New Testament I actually put myself as the writer which helps to answer the questions of the who, what, why, when and where. Because as I'm imagining myself as the writer, I'm asking myself those pertinent questions of the who, when, what, why and where. This will help to make scriptures more than just mere words, and a lot of new revelation will start coming about.

Imagine the Holy Spirit inside of yourself. I do this by choosing one of the representations of Holy Spirit. He is represented as water, oil, fire, air/breath. Each one of these things have specific sounds that they make for example *"out of the belly flows rivers of living water"*.

> **38** Believe in me so that rivers of living water will burst out from within you, flowing from your innermost being, just like the Scripture says! (John 7:38, TPT)

Imagine water moving around inside of you from your belly to your toes, up from your belly to your throat and out of your mouth where He becomes your very breath. As rivers make a sound so does the Holy Spirit as water. Since there is sound as he goes out of your mouth, as water, that sound becomes words. So, just let the words flow out of you. This scenario is also helpful when wanting to speak in tongues. Or it can be adapted to healing or even communicating with Holy Spirit without verbal communication. As he's sounding like a roaring river what is he saying? Holy Spirit appeared to Moses as a burning bush through which he talked to Moses. Imagine flames of fire inside of your chest, fire makes a crackling sound. What is he speaking to you through the crackling sound? These are just some examples, to get you started. As you practice this, Holy Spirit will become more real to you, and you will have more awareness of His presence inside of you at all times.

Imagine yourself doing supernatural works! Of course, this corresponds with imagining yourself walking with Jesus in the Gospels. You can also use your imagination in your daily life, with a supernatural twist. If you're running late to an appointment or in getting to your job, why not imagine suddenly being whisked away by the Holy Spirit while driving your car? All of a sudden you and your car arrive at your destination. I have literally experienced that before. A work associate cuts themself, imagine you walking up to them and speaking words of life and all of the sudden the wound stops bleeding and is sealed up. Then go do it! You lock your keys in the car, use your imagination and see the car being unlocked seemingly by itself. But you know the Holy Spirit as air so he is going into the vehicle and unlocking it. There are many different scenarios you can use. All of these things completely line up with a scripture we mentioned earlier.

> **6** Don't be pulled in different directions or worried about a thing. Be saturated in prayer throughout each day, offering your faith-filled requests before God **with overflowing gratitude. Tell him every detail of your life, 7 then God's wonderful peace that transcends human understanding**, will make the answers known to you through Jesus Christ. **8** So keep your thoughts continually fixed on all that is authentic and real, honorable and admirable, beautiful and respectful, pure and holy, merciful and kind. **And fasten your thoughts on every glorious work of God, praising him always. 9** Follow the example of all that we have imparted to you and the God of peace will be with you in all things. (Philippians 4:6-9, TPT)

There is a cautionary note that comes with this.

> **18** Don't let anyone disqualify you from your prize! Don't let their pretended sincerity fool you as they deliberately **lead you into their initiation of angel worship.** For they take pleasure in pretending **to be experts of something they know nothing about.** Their reasoning is meaningless and comes only from their own opinions. **19 They refuse to take hold of the true source. But we receive directly from him, and his life supplies vitality into every part of his body** through the joining ligaments connecting us all as one. He is the divine Head who guides his body and causes it to grow **by the supernatural power of God.** (Colossians 2:18-19, TPT)

Angels are ministering spirits and they have a part to play but I never have and never will recommend including angels in the use of imagination. If there is a need for me to have interaction with an angel, then I let Holy Spirit initiate it with a dream or vision. I don't seek contact with angels. And I don't imagine them having a part of healing or the supernatural. Nor do I imagine what heaven is like or visiting heaven, once again I believe that God will initiate such things. Notice in the above scripture "They refuse to take hold of the true source" and "we receive directly from him, and his life supplies vitality into every part of his body". Leave well enough alone and let the Holy Spirit deal with these things.

Speak in tongues often:

Speaking in tongues is huge and a huge part of my daily life. In reference this is speaking in tongues as a private prayer language. In every book of mine there is a mention of this, and perhaps one day I'll write a book specifically about speaking in tongues. As a private prayer language, it is the means that Holy Spirit uses to edify the inner man, and to reveal things to us we possibly couldn't understand any other way. Speak in tongues while driving to work, during quiet time, as often as you're able. The benefits of it will be obvious the more you practice this.

Quiet your thoughts:

Take time away from planning your life out, and from worrying about what is going on in your busy life. Instead just take time to quiet your thoughts and focus on the Holy Spirit inside of you. Many of the other suggestions can apply to your quiet time. Go into a room in the house that no one else is in or take a walk and think only thoughts of the Lord. Even if you just sit quietly with only thoughts of Holy Spirit in you and around you. Get rid of all that internal chatter and just sit quietly or even take this time to imagine what the Holy Spirit inside of you really means. You can have music softly playing in the background as long as the music itself doesn't distract you.

Act on an impulse to help another person:

When you feel a nudge to go out of your way to speak a blessing to another person, just do it. Look for opportunities to tell a person a quick testimony of what Jesus has done for you. Give an encouraging word to someone else. Don't think about what you're going to say, just walk up to a person and let the words come out. This often impulsively leads to giving a gift of the Holy Spirit through a prophetic word, word of wisdom, healing or one of the other gifts. Just be open and looking for opportunities to bless a person. In fact, even saying "bless you" to anyone can be a huge gift for many people. Often, I will purposefully open a door for someone just to say "bless you", just that one impulsive act has led to experiencing the supernatural.

Just today, I received an email from a person who I met at a bar years ago. I felt a nudging from the Holy Spirit to pull into this bar. I walked inside and there was a fella who needed cheering up, he was at a low point in his life, both physically and mentally. We struck up a conversation which ended up with me giving him several words of knowledge, words of wisdom, and I gave him the gift of healing. His back was healed right there at the bar. All of this had an influence on him so he felt the need to look me up on the internet and send me an email many years later. He was just grateful that I took the time to encourage him. He stated that that one act of kindness has changed his life. That's what happens when we listen to the gentle impulses of the Holy Spirit and are open to these types of experiences.

Worksheet: Chapter: 12

1. Name five ways to increase your awareness of the Holy Spirit in you.

____
____
____
____
____

2. Commit yourself to self-study of the Bible. Name a couple of ways you can change the way you study scriptures, that will help gain a better understanding of them.

____
____
____
____
____
____

3. What are three practices you can do to increase the use of your imagination, in a way that will cause you to experience the supernatural?

____
____
____
____

4. Name two benefits from speaking in tongues.

5. What are the cautions when it comes to using your imagination?

6. Name two times an impulsive act led to a life changing encounter with another person.

7. The more awareness we have of Christ in us, the more supernatural encounters we will have. Name a couple of lifestyle changes that can promote this to occur?

13. Operations in the gifts

I'm sitting here drinking my coffee and thinking about a lot of different things. We've discussed how we have the Holy Spirit who is the Gift and the anointing, we should and can be walking in the supernatural in every area of our personal lives. As we mature, we should experience this more, and shouldn't have to seek out another person for words from God (He is in us), or for healing, or for any other need. I really want you, my friends, to understand this. This is not about being self-reliant it is about being reliant on Holy Spirit. Nor is it being a recluse, that's where the gifts of the Holy Spirit come in as we've already discussed. The gifts are for the people we interact with every day and vary according to the need of the person we're interacting with, as previously taught. There is a need for the gifts to be in operation during church services, there is no denying that. However, we should be giving the gifts away in our everyday lives. While we're at work, doing grocery shopping, enjoying a meal at a restaurant, wherever we're at. This is how we spread God's Kingdom. Instead of judging people by their looks or actions we should be giving them a gift so they come to accept Jesus, and then can start walking in a personal relationship.

Christians, as a majority, go about the Gospel in a completely wrong way. In fact, it was the common way of doing it that kept me an atheist for forty something years. Walking up to someone asking them if they know Jesus and telling them that if they don't know Jesus they're going to hell, then spewing out bible scriptures is completely the wrong way to go about the Gospel. This creates more atheists and will drive unbelievers away. By the way spewing scriptures out saying, "the bible says", will likely offend unbelievers, the bible isn't their guide to begin with. Jesus did not offend unbelievers, he offended those who claimed to know God (the Pharisees). The "sinners" loved Jesus because he reached out with love, not with condemnation. Bible tracts are just as offensive. Our goal shouldn't be to get people into your church, although when you approach a person in love that could happen. But that shouldn't be your goal. The goal is to introduce them to Jesus who loves them, not to a religious organization.

Remember, Jesus in the gospels was talking to a people already in a religious organization. The children of Israel were Jews, that was the only religious system available for them. He was at that time sent only to the children of Israel, so our approach to them should be somewhat different. When Peter gave his speech, which had harsh language in it, he was in Jerusalem so his harsh tone was directed specifically to them. Once again, it's a matter of who in this case Peter was talking to.

> **12** With the crowd surrounding him, Peter said to them all, "People of Israel, listen to me! Why are you so amazed by this healing? Why do you stare at us? We didn't make this crippled man walk by our own power or authority. **13** The God of our ancestors, Abraham, Isaac, and Jacob, has done

> this. **For he has glorified his Servant Jesus, the one you denied to Pilate's face when he decided to release him—and you insisted that he be crucified. 14 You rejected the one who is holy and righteous, and instead begged for a murderer to be released. 15 You killed the Prince of Life!** But God raised him from the dead, and we stand here as witnesses to that fact. (Acts 3:12-15, TPT)

This does not apply to any of us living today, so standing up on a street corner hollering and screaming 'you're going to hell' is the wrong approach and is ineffective. Likewise, just as ineffective and offensive is handing out bible tracts essentially saying the same thing. The whole reason we have the gifts to give away is to draw people to a Loving Father, and to Jesus and show them the power of a personal relationship with them. We think the gospel is preaching 'conform to a religious organization or go to hell' but that just isn't the gospel. The GOOD NEWS is that when we accept Jesus as Lord and savior, we then are citizens of the kingdom of God as sons and daughters of a Loving Father! Now that's Good News! Add to that giving them a free gift that changes their life such as a healing. Now that is life changing and indeed something to celebrate about.

Here in the bible belt, those who work in restaurants as waiters, waitresses, cooks and managers hate the Sunday Church crowd. They are obnoxious, rude, condescending, judgmental and tip very little. How much of a change would there be if the Sunday church crowd actually operated in giving the gifts of the Holy Spirit to these servers, waiters and waitresses? Let's now go over the nine gifts you can give to others:

1. The word of knowledge

2. Word of Wisdom
3. A prophetic word
4. The gift of faith
5. The gift of healing
6. working miracles
7. Discerning of spirits
8. Different types of tongues
9. Interpretation of tongues

The word of knowledge:

Remember that you already have access to all of the gifts for your personal life, so what I'm describing in all these gifts applies to yourself as well. But in this case, I'm talking about giving these gifts to someone else. The word of knowledge is telling someone something about their life that you couldn't know otherwise. It is God's perfect knowledge about a situation in their life they need a solution for or it's also a word that God will use as a confirmation to that person. This can range anywhere from telling a person where their missing car keys are, to, they have three cats and one of them is blind. Telling them that they have three cats and one is blind would lead you directly into giving the person the gift of a healing, because right there you would pray for their blind cat. Another example would be giving a word about a health condition that isn't obvious. For example: your right knee catches when you bend over and then you experience a sharp pain. This will also directly lead you to pray for them and see them healed.

As a word of confirmation, it could be something as simple as Jesus did, He was giving the woman at the well a word of knowledge when He stated that she had had five husbands and living with a man that wasn't her husband.

> **17** "But I'm not married," the woman answered. "That's true," Jesus said, **18** "for you've been married five times and now you're living with a man who is not your husband. You have told the truth." (John 4:17-18, TPT)

That confirmed to her that Jesus was a prophet and that He spoke Truth, and then she had the revelation that He was the Messiah. There are many different ways the Lord uses a word of knowledge to speak to a person. Often, it's a Holy Spirit set up that leads to giving other gifts to that person. The weirdest word of knowledge I've received was that this person had a green hose that had a cut in it and was leaking water. It was in their backyard and was attached to a single water line coming up from the ground. She then called her husband and found out that it was correct. Oftentimes it can be confusing whether it's a word of knowledge, word of wisdom or prophetic word. Don't spend time trying to figure what specific gift it is.

The Holy Spirit can give you a word of knowledge by various ways, an image, a picture, words or just knowing. The key is not to rationalize it or try to figure out the meaning. The word was for that specific person and it will make sense to them. In the case of the green water hose, I just described what I saw without adding anything to it.

Word of Wisdom:

A word of wisdom is giving guidance from Holy Spirit to a person to solve a specific problem. This often entails Holy Spirit showing you the specific problem or event that will happen to this person in the future. You are giving God's Wisdom in handling this problem. This can often come as a warning to that person, but with this word should come peace and a resolution. The perfect example of a word of wisdom is when the two mothers came, and the dispute was who the real mother was.

> **23** Then the king said, "Let's get the facts straight. Both of you claim the living child is yours, and each says that the dead one belongs to the other. **24** All right, bring me a sword." So a sword was brought to the king.**25** Then he said, "Cut the living child in two, and give half to one woman and half to the other!"**26** Then the woman who was the real mother of the living child, and who loved him very much, cried out, "Oh no, my lord! Give her the child—please do not kill him!" But the other woman said, "All right, he will be neither yours nor mine; divide him between us!" **27**Then the king said, "Do not kill the child, but give him to the woman who wants him to live, for she is his mother!" **28** When all Israel heard the king's decision, the people were in awe of the king, for they saw the wisdom God had given him for rendering justice. (1 Kings 3:23-28, NLT)

The king was given a word of wisdom from God, on how to handle the situation. Another example is with Jesus instructing the disciples on how to acquire the donkey for him in regard to Palm Sunday.

> **2** "Go into the village over there," he said. "As soon as you enter it, you will see a donkey tied there, with its colt beside it. Untie them and bring them to me. **3** If anyone asks what you are doing, just say, 'The Lord needs them,' and he will immediately let you take them." (Matthew 21:2-3, NLT)

This is what words of wisdom are all about, and usually they are about a future situation. Which is why prophetic words and words of wisdom are so often confused. But often all three words are combined together when giving these gifts to a person. Another way to define words of wisdom is guidance on the steps to take on specific situation. They can involve any area of a person's life. It is important to know that these words are directly from the Holy Spirit and not from the rational mind, a lot of damage can be done to a person if it is simply human wisdom. Which is why the words of knowledge, wisdom and prophetic work so closely together. God gives you knowledge of something that otherwise you would know nothing about, then he gives you wisdom on how to guide the person to the resolution and at the same time gives you a word to encourage, motivate and comfort them, which is the prophetic word. One way to test the word is that it will be very specific beyond what you could come up with on your own, and the resolution would not be something that you would normally advise another person. For instance, with King Solomon, very few of us would have come up with the solution that he did.

The Prophetic Word:

In my opinion this is the most misunderstood, gift of all. People use prophecy as if the only point of it is predicting the future, that isn't true. Others use prophecy with a harshness, because they are going by the Old Covenant examples of prophecy. Prophecy is a word given to encourage, strengthen and comfort.

> **1** Let love be your highest goal! But you should also desire the special abilities the Spirit gives—especially the ability to prophesy. **2** For if you have the ability to speak in tongues, you will be talking only to God, since people won't be able to understand you. You will be speaking by the power of the Spirit, but it will all be mysterious. **3 But one who prophesies strengthens others, encourages them, and**

> **comforts them. 4** A person who speaks in tongues is strengthened personally, but one who speaks a word of prophecy strengthens the entire church. **5** I wish you could all speak in tongues, **but even more I wish you could all prophesy.** For prophecy is greater than speaking in tongues, unless someone interprets what you are saying so that the whole church will be strengthened. (1 Corinthians 14:1-5, TPT)

Prophecy in the New Covenant looks different than in the Old Covenant. Most of the prophecies in the Old Covenant were warnings to the children of Israel or prophesying about the coming of the Messiah. In the New Covenant it is meant to strengthen, encourage and comfort. It is not meant to be harsh words, it can at times be a correction, but stated in a way that strengthens a person. As soon as I hear a so-called prophet being harsh, or doom and gloom especially if they are speaking Old English KJV style, I literally stop listening to them. Any person can prophesy they don't need to call themselves a prophet or hold the office of a prophet. Notice that Paul states that he desires that all could prophesy. The end result of a prophetic word should be one that strengthens, encourages and comforts. This can include telling of a past event, a present circumstance and a prediction of the future, but the focus shouldn't be on these things. A good solid word of prophecy should not put the focus on the one giving the word, it should lead the person straight to Jesus. Nor does it have to be long and drawn out. If a prophetic word lasts longer than 3 or 4 minutes, I hit the snooze button and am no longer listening. Also understand I'm using this in the context of a prophetic word to an individual outside of a church.

> **31** On the way, Jesus told them, "Tonight all of you will desert me. For the Scriptures say, 'God will strike the Shepherd, and the sheep of the flock will be scattered.' **32**

> But after I have been raised from the dead, I will go ahead of you to Galilee and meet you there." (Matthew 26:31-32, NLT)

This prophetic word from Jesus to the Apostles is a good example of a negative circumstance and how Jesus did not give it in a condemning doom and gloom way. He stated what was going to happen, to strengthen the disciples when it happened. Then offered comfort in saying "*I will go ahead of you to Galilee and meet you there.*" Of course, this example is a fulfillment of scripture, but it is a great example of how to give a word of prophecy to individuals. It was short, simple direct: but as the events played out was a huge comfort to the disciples. Prophecy does often include negative circumstances, but it should always leave the person encouraged.

In receiving a prophetic word, always ask the Lord for confirmation. Don't just accept a prophetic word at face value. The prophetic word can be a huge blessing, but it can also have a huge negative impact. There should be a confirmation from the Holy Spirit from deep within.

A short example from my own experience is that the Lord showed me that this person had lost his job. But a perfect stranger would approach him in two weeks with a job offer. He would know this was the position for him, because the one offering the position would say "God Bless you". A few weeks later this man came back and confirmed that this had happened.

The gift of faith:

This gift I see as two different uses. Which differs from most views on this gift. The common viewpoint is a sudden burst of extraordinary faith in a circumstance when it is needed. A good example of this would be with Stephen when he was being stoned to death.

> **55** But Stephen, **overtaken with great faith**, was full of the Holy Spirit. He fixed his gaze into the heavenly realm and saw the glory and splendor of God—and Jesus, who stood up at the right hand of God. (Acts 7:55, TPT)

However, I somewhat question this because as believers we each have the measure of faith and the spirit of faith who is the Holy Spirit. So, while I do see the common belief about the gift of faith as being true, I also see another side that accompanies the gift of faith. I also see the gift of faith as being given to an unbeliever so that person can accept Christ. Faith is a gift from God, so I believe that this gift is in action when a person accepts Christ. After salvation happens, we have all the faith we need in the form of Holy Spirit.

> **13 We have the same Spirit of faith** that is described in the Scriptures when it says,"First I believed, then I spoke in faith." **So we also first believe then speak in faith.** (2 Corinthians 4:13, TPT)

> **8** For by grace are ye saved **through faith**; and that not of yourselves**: it is the gift of God**: (Ephesians 2:8, KJV)

So, I believe that this gift is two-fold, it is correct to say that it's a sudden burst of faith, but also it is the gift we receive when we first believe in Christ. An example of each one of these uses are as a sudden burst of faith, was when I saw a woman raised from the dead. Then a person receiving the gift of faith by believing in Christ was a young man in the hospital dying from sepsis, he both accepted Christ and received a new heart (the organ).

The gifts of healing:

This one is obvious it is healing whether physically, or emotionally. I want to be perfectly clear; every single believer can give any of these gifts to another person. No one "special person" is an anointed healer. We all are to give the gifts of healing to other people.

> **15** And he said to them, "As you go into all the world, preach openly the wonderful news of the gospel to the entire human race! **16** Whoever believes the good news and is baptized will be saved, and whoever does not believe the good news will be condemned. **17 And these miracle signs will accompany those who believe:** They will drive out demons in the power of my name. They will speak in tongues. **18** They will be supernaturally protected from snakes and from drinking anything poisonous. **And they will lay hands on the sick and heal them."** (Mark 16:15-18 TPT)

Scriptures are perfectly clear on this, there is a belief that only certain anointed people can see healings. This is not true, any believer of Christ can and should heal others (see 'Unlocking the Mystery of Divine Healing'). There is also the belief that one person has a "special" anointing over certain illnesses. This is a wrong theology based only on observation, not scriptures. People think that because a person was healed from Lou Gehrig's that they have a "special anointing" to heal those with Lou Gehrig's disease. Now granted because I was healed from Lou Gehrig's, I will have a greater expectation for that condition to be healed, than others may have. But the disciples and the other seventy healed all manner of illnesses. No one was ever singled out with a "special anointing" over specific diseases. We, as the body of Christ, need to get rid of that theology. I've seen nearly every single disease healed, not just the one. Let's not put God in a box and limit him. I could really go off on many tangents with this one, but that's why I've got three books on this very subject. Time for a coffee break, then we'll get into the remaining gifts.

The working of miracles:

The definition of a miracle is an extreme event with divine intervention in human affairs. It can include anything. In scriptures it includes everything from parting the Red Sea, to walking on water. Once again, we are citizens of the supernatural kingdom of God, so the working of miracles should be an everyday part of life. The loving Father wants all of our needs met and wants us to meet the needs of other people. If we come across a person who has locked their keys in the car, command the car to be unlocked.

> **14** Ask me anything in my name, and I will do it for you!" (John 14:14, TPT)
>
> **12** "I tell you this timeless truth: The person who follows me in faith, believing in me, will do the same mighty miracles that I do—even greater miracles than these because I go to be with my Father! (John 14:12, TPT)

Discerning of spirits:

This gift is discerning whether a person is operating from the Spirit of God or of the world. This gift is actually used a lot more than what people think. This gift is not mind reading, psychic phenomena, or the ability to find fault and to criticize. It is really spiritual insight and is meant to guide and protect believers. The Holy Spirit bears witness within us to tell us whether something is or isn't from God. There are also three ways to determine if someone is from God.

Observing the fruit by a person's conduct or actions, we will know whether they are of God by their fruit.

> **15** "Constantly be on your guard against phony prophets. They come disguised as lambs, appearing to be genuine, but

> on the inside they are like wild, ravenous wolves! **16** You can spot them by their actions, for the fruits of their character will be obvious. You won't find sweet grapes hanging on a thorn bush, and you'll never pick good fruit from a tumbleweed. **17–19** So if the tree is good, it will produce good fruit; but if the tree is bad, it will bear only rotten fruit and it deserves to be cut down and burned. **20** Look at the obvious fruit of their lives and ministries, and then you'll know whether they are true or false." (Matthew 7:15-20, TPT)

Observing whether they exalt Jesus as Lord and Savior.

> **3** Therefore, I want to impart to you an understanding of the following: No one speaking by the Spirit of God would ever say, "Jesus is the accursed one." No one can say, "Jesus is the Lord Yahweh," unless the Holy Spirit is speaking through him. (1 Corinthians 12:3 TPT)

By listening to what a person says. This one is specifically talking about false prophets.

> **1** Delightfully loved friends, don't trust every spirit, but carefully examine what they say to determine if they are of God, because many false prophets have mingled into the world. **2** Here's the test for those with the genuine Spirit of God: they will confess Jesus as the Christ who has come in the flesh. **3** Everyone who does not acknowledge that Jesus is from God has the spirit of antichrist, which you heard was coming and is already active in the world. (1 John 4:1-3, TPT)

There are many examples of Jesus using discerning of spirits.

> **15** Then the Pharisees came together to make a plan to entrap Jesus with his own words. **16** So they sent some of their disciples together with some staunch supporters of Herod. They said to Jesus, "Teacher, we know that you're an honest man of integrity and you teach us the truth of God's ways. We can clearly see that you're not one who speaks only to win the people's favor, because you speak the truth without regard to the consequences. **17** So tell us, then, what you think. Is it proper for us Jews to pay taxes to Caesar or not?" **18** Jesus knew the malice that was hidden behind their cunning ploy and said, "Why are you testing me, you imposters who think you have all the answers? (Matthew 22:15-18, TPT)

There has been more than one occasion that a person posing as being genuine has tried to set me up. But through the gift of discerning of spirits I was able to see through it and avoid the trap set. Thank you, Jesus!

The gift of tongues:

There are three types of tongues of God, of angels and of men. The tongues of God are our private prayer language, which also includes singing in tongues as worship. This type of tongues edifies our inner man, is also used to bring about personal revelations, and as a means of worship. This type of tongues is also used for intercession for others. This should be the most used gift of tongues in every believer's life.

> **2** For if you have the ability to speak in tongues, you will be talking only to God, since people won't be able to understand you. You will be speaking by the power of the Spirit, but it will all be mysterious. (1 Corinthians 14:2, NLT)

The tongue of men is a known foreign language that you've never been taught. This tongue is the one that is a sign for unbelievers.

> **6** When they heard the loud noise, everyone came running, and they were bewildered to hear their own languages being spoken by the believers. (Acts 2:6, NLT)

The tongues of angels are meant for the edification of a body of believers and is made known by interpretation.

> **5** I wish you could all speak in tongues, but even more I wish you could all prophesy. For prophecy is greater than speaking in tongues, unless someone interprets what you are saying so that the whole church will be strengthened. (1 Corinthians 14:5, NLT)

Interpretation of tongues:

The most common usage of this gift is in a church setting for interpretation of the tongues of angels, however, I often ask for the interpretation of my prayer language while reading scriptures. A lot of my revelations have come from speaking in the tongues of God while reading scriptures and asking Holy Spirit to convey to me the meaning.

All of the gifts are meant for the benefits of others throughout our daily lives so we should be using the gifts often. They are available to us and meant to be used abundantly. When approaching people be respectful and always operate in love. If you have a prophetic word or word of wisdom it is my opinion that it should be presented in a way that is not demanding or arrogant. By that I mean you should say "I feel the Lord is saying" then you give the word. Let them decide for themselves whether it has merit or not. The wrong approach would be to say "The Lord has commanded you to listen and do what I say". When you approach someone in a public place and they are a stranger to you, take time for casual conversation. It doesn't have to be a thirty-minute conversation, just long enough for them to trust you. Often this will give you the opportunity to give the gift to them. You don't even have to give them a "thus saith the Lord". They will know in their hearts that it is from him, whether you specify it or not. Using these gifts should not cause the person embarrassment, rather it should build them up. Be casual, friendly, respectful and loving. It isn't about making a reputation, it's not about you, it's about giving them a gift from a loving Heavenly Father.

Worksheet: Chapter 13

1. Which of the nine gifts would be used to give guidance on a specific circumstance in someone's life? Why?

____

____

2. Which of the nine gifts would be a fact given about a person that you have no prior knowledge of?

____

____

3. Which gift should always be accompanied by an interpretation?

____

____

4. Describe two different scenarios that the gift of faith could be given?

____

____

____

____

____

5. When it comes to the gift of healing, describe how you would approach a person.

____

____

____

____

6. Define the discerning of spirits.

____

____

____

____

7. How should you always act towards other people?

____

____

____

14. Naturally Supernatural

> **2** Stop imitating the ideals and opinions of the culture around you, but be inwardly transformed by the **Holy Spirit through a total reformation of how you think**. This will empower you to discern God's will as you live a beautiful life, satisfying and perfect in his eyes. (Roman 12:2, TPT)

We are citizens of God's Kingdom. Therefore, we should act accordingly. We should be operating from the Holy Spirit in all our ways. We should stand out in a crowd of people because our actions reflect Jesus and the Love of God. Our words should reflect this as well, we should be living our lives not as human beings, but as spiritual beings who represent God's Kingdom. The supernatural should become natural and we can operate out of the Joy of the Lord in all circumstances, not out of fear. With the Holy Spirit living inside of us we are far more than mere mortals.

> **7** For God will never give you the spirit of fear, **but the Holy Spirit who gives you mighty power, love, and self-control. 8** So never be ashamed of the testimony of our Lord, nor be embarrassed over my imprisonment, **but overcome every evil by the revelation of the power of God!** (2 Timothy 1:7-8, TPT)

For far too long the majority of the body of believers have totally ignored the power of God that we have within our grasp. Many of us have led lives that haven't reflected the citizenship of heaven that we have. Our interpretation of scriptures has left out the power of God that is available for every believer. It is time to start living out the truest form of salvation that will impact every person we come into contact with, so that they will want what we have for themselves.

This book was written so that the boundaries that we have placed upon believers in Christ are broken and we start living up to the potential that we all have available. I confidentially expect that this has fired up your imagination and you look at the life we have In Christ with a fresh perspective and with a zeal that cannot be quenched. We all face trials and periods of hardship, but with Holy Spirit in us and a greater harmony in the body of Christ, those hardships shall pass away and we will start living as unwavering supernatural sons and daughters of Our Heavenly Father.

Therefore, I challenge all believers to ask Holy Spirit throughout the day, for wisdom and knowledge when issues come up. He will answer, include Him in your daily lives. Let Him be your problem solver. Time for me to put my feet up on the desk and enjoy the flavor of my cup of coffee! God Bless you!

Worksheet: Chapter 14

1. What are some beliefs that you previously had that changed during the reading of this book?

____

____

____

____

2. Name what changed in your life as a result of reading this book.

____

____

____

____

3. Record a supernatural experience that you've had since finishing the book.

____

____

____

____

4. What information in the book most fascinated you?

____

____

____

____

____

5. Combine your answers from the above questions into a review of why you would recommend this book.

____

____

____

____

Now, please submit this to Amazon as a book review, and thank you!

Be Blessed, Be healed, Be a supernatural Blessing!

About the Author

Tony Myers is author of the books "The Lord Jesus Healed Me" and "Unlocking the Mystery of Diving Healing" and "Knocking Food Off Its Pedestal". He lives in Virginia with his precious wife Deb and all their four-legged family members. A former atheist who was healed from Lou Gehrig's disease, this illness left him paralyzed and dying. Then, he was suddenly healed by Christ.

Since his healing on July 4th, 2012; He has appeared as a guest on many different platforms and media. This includes radio, television, and of course the internet. His testimony was featured on the 700 Club in April, 2019. Most of his time is spent on his business and ministering the Gospel of Christ to others. The planned future holds more speaking engagements and more books to come. Tony is very open to be contacted for prayer, ministry, book signings, and for opportunities to preach the Gospel of Christ.

Contact information

Website: tonybelieves.com – email tonyjustbelieves@gmail.com

More from Tony

After living a life of atheism, Tony Myers was fighting for his life. He was completely paralyzed, and his body was shutting down. Diagnosed with Lou Gehrig's disease, a debilitating neurological disease with no cure or treatment options, all hope was lost. Then suddenly one day, Tony, determined to end his own life, found a miracle healing instead! During this journey you will cry, laugh, feel his wife's heartache, and then finally have a tremendous burst of joy as you celebrate his miracle with him and his wife Deb. Tony's honest, folksy telling of his story will make you believe he's sitting right in front of you drinking coffee! This story will encourage, motivate, and inspire you to believe in a miracle for yourself. If you are need of hope and encouragement, then this book is for you.

This book is the field manual as far as receiving healing for yourself is concerned. It is meant to awaken in the readers the mind of Christ and help them tap into the God-realm (i.e., "kingdom of heaven"). That's where we can receive the riches of Christ provided to us by grace, specifically, divine health and healing.

Divine healing from the comfort of your home? Is that truly possible? The problem isn't getting new information. The problem is getting what's already available to work for you. Over many centuries, the simple message of the cross has been obscured and diluted by many religious and secular traditions. And that's exactly why and where this book comes in. Its purpose is to get you to see the simple truth of the Gospel as it's related to divine healing and health, without any unnecessary additives. This book is written in a simple, conversational style. It takes you from the garden of Eden all the way to the present day. It shows you how the revelation about divine healing and health was offered by God, and how and why it kept on getting ignored and put aside. Most importantly, this book shows you what you can do to recover God's blueprint for your own health and how you can get the Gospel truth about divine healing to work for you from the comfort of your home.

In this book, Tony Myers tackles tough issues related to food, our perceptions of food, and how to attain a healthy, supernatural life through simple practices and a fresh perspective of the things that go in our mouths. You'll learn how to avoid the pitfalls that keep you from healthy living from God's point of view and be able to correct the misinformation we've received along the way

Before you close this book, please go to Amazon and leave a review. Thank you very much!

85-86 - Story

Made in the USA
Monee, IL
05 October 2020